ALSO BY DAVID LEBEDOFF

THE UNCIVIL WAR

CLEANING UP

THE NEW ELITE

WARD NUMBER SIX

THE 21ST BALLOT

THE SAME MAN

The

SAME MAN

–

GEORGE ORWELL

AND EVELYN WAUGH

IN LOVE AND WAR

David Lebedoff

RANDOM HOUSE | NEW YORK

Published in the United States by Random House,
an imprint of The Random House Publishing Group,
a division of Random House, Inc., New York.

RANDOM HOUSE and colophon are registered
trademarks of Random House, Inc.

Title page photographs: Waugh photo by
Mark Gerson / Camera Press / Retna; Orwell photo by
Vernon Richards / George Orwell Archive, UCL Library
Services, Special Collections

LIBRARY OF CONGRESS
CATALOGING-IN-PUBLICATION DATA
Lebedoff, David.
The same man : George Orwell and Evelyn Waugh
in love and war / David Lebedoff.
p.   cm.
ISBN 978-1-4000-6634-6
1. Orwell, George, 1903–1950. 2. Waugh, Evelyn,
1903–1966. 3. Authors, English—20th century—
Biography. I. Title.
PR6029.R8Z7198 2008
828'.91209—dc22   2007038422

Printed in the United States of America on acid-free paper

www.randomhouse.com

2 4 6 8 9 7 5 3 1

FIRST EDITION

Book design by Barbara M. Bachman

For

HAROLD W. CHASE

1922-1982

CONTENTS

-

PROLOGUE

-

ON A CLOUDLESS NIGHT IN JUNE 1930, AT THE HEIGHT OF a brilliant London season, the Duke and Duchess of Marlborough were giving a dinner party at their splendid house in town. At the revels of younger hosts, the lilt of Gershwin would reach out into the cobbled streets to lure any stragglers inside.

But not at this party. No saxophones for the Marlboroughs. Here, the guests were the entertainment, a reliable mixture of ancient rank and current fame. Across the street a small crowd felt itself fortunate to be allowed to watch the swells arrive.

One of those for whom the great door opened was a famous author, though only twenty-six years old. He was short, but carried himself like a guardsman as he strode through the entry hall. Robust, florid, and compact, he owed his attractiveness to fine features and personal magnetism. All the men present were in white tie, but small tweaks of taste were tolerated, and the elegant young author received glances of approval as he made his way upstream.

He was Evelyn Waugh, and he had written two successful comic novels; the second, *Vile Bodies*, was the talk of the town, the town inhabited largely by the sort of people who were gathered at the Marlboroughs' that evening.

Waugh was in the habit of keeping a diary, much of which was carefully devoted to recording precisely this type of event. So we know today how his evening proceeded. He was seated at dinner next to Edith Sitwell, another writer, less in vogue at the moment but with a noble pedigree.

During the course of the evening she was approached by the opera star Nellie Melba, who gushed, "I read your books, Miss Sitwell."

"If it comes to that, Dame Melba [*sic*], I have heard you sing," replied Sitwell, who was to become a dame herself. It was that kind of party.

And all its glitter went into the diary: "There were two ambassadors and about forty hard-faced middle-aged peers and peeresses. The Duchess very battered with fine diamonds. The Duke wearing the Garter: also a vast silk turban over bandaged eyes from which his little hook nose protruded. When I left, the Duchess said, 'Oh, you are like Marlborough. He has such a mundane mind. He will go to any party for which he is sent a printed invitation.' "

Right she was. The young author then went on to another party, which ended up in the diary, too.

Others might have taken the duchess's comments as unflattering, but the diarist was careful to preserve them, because they put him on equal footing with a duke.

For Evelyn Waugh, the toast of the hosts who mattered, this had been a typical evening in a typical week. The following day he recorded he had "Lunched at the Ritz. Met Noel Coward." All the pages of the diary were filled with glittering names and places—Lady Cunard, Randolph Churchill (who "threw a cocktail in Wanda's face"), Nancy Mitford, Cecil Beaton, Diana Guinness, Lord Birkenhead, Lady Ponsonby, Sophie Tucker (!), Lord David Cecil, Harold Nicholson, and on and on. A picnic: "Diana Cavendish, three Cecil boys and two Ormsby-Gore children." "The party at tea was Lady Oxford, Lady Clifford, Lady Russell, John Buchan and the Prime Minister." Waugh's diary wasn't so much a record as a scorecard. It was a list of each goal made. Through these notations he was assuring posterity and himself that he had become just who he had wanted to be.

It had not been easy to join up with these gods. His new life did not reflect his origins. He had soared on wings of will.

ON THAT SAME BALMY NIGHT in June of 1930, while Waugh was amusing the duchess, a young man of the same age but very different appearance, Eric Blair, was working alone in a small, shabby room in the working-class section of Leeds, a manufacturing city in the north. He was the unwelcome guest of his brother-in-law, who regarded this lodger as a penniless failure with no job and no future.

This opinion was shared by almost everyone acquainted with Blair. It was a relatively small group but one that included several experts on failure; they had learned about it firsthand. Blair looked, and often smelled, like a tramp, because he was one. He, however, made the distinction that he wasn't really a tramp, but only chose to *be among* tramps to free himself from class prejudices about poverty and dirt. He put it this way: "When you have shared a bed with a tramp and drunk tea out of the same snuff-tin, you feel that you have seen the worst and the worst has no terrors for you."

In pursuit of this freedom from class prejudice, he would

dress in rags and disappear for days or weeks—not just to the slums of London but to towns throughout the countryside. Then he would return to his parents' small house or the apartment of a friend. He had no home of his own.

This was why he was staying with his brother-in-law in Leeds. He couldn't remain on the road forever. He needed peace and quiet. He was writing a book.

He was writing a book about restaurants in France, but it was no tourist guide. In fact, it probably made its readers want to eat at home. It was the tale of Blair's labors during the previous two years in the filthy commercial kitchens of Paris, cleaning the dishes of rich diners on the other side of the swinging door. This was not the same as tramping to learn tolerance. It was hard work amid dirt and slops and noise to earn enough to stay alive. Blair's proposed book was the angry memory of a sick and hungry man scraping the leavings of the rich. He wanted to write about how the very poorest lived.

So now, every evening in Leeds, he would finish supper with his sister and her husband, go up to his small room, and type away throughout the night. (The clattering must have driven his brother-in-law mad.) He worked and worked to get the words right. His progress was difficult and slow.

Blair thought of himself as a writer, though he had little evidence to support that. Though the same age as Waugh, he had yet to produce a book. He had attempted fiction and finished a few articles, but almost all of them were rejected. One of the few he managed to publish, in a small London magazine, just about the time of the Marlborough dinner party, was a review of Edith Sitwell's book on Alexander Pope. He praised her work but years later was still trying to find a way actually to meet Waugh's renowned dinner partner.

The grim typist in the attic struggling to find an audience and the celebrated author laughing amid the lords of the land could not have seemed less alike. Waugh was hard and funny and elegant, while Blair seemed soft and quiet and shabby. Each had staked out opposite ends of the social ladder and already looked their parts. One resembled the embodiment of privilege, and the other its emaciated foe. Even their heights were a contrast; Blair was six foot three and Waugh just barely five foot six.

They would always lead completely different lives. But they both would devote those lives to writing. And though they wrote for different readers and in different voices, they left us a shared vision of their own time, and ours.

Today, George Orwell's essays and some of his novels and Waugh's body of fiction are considered masterworks. It is easy now to claim these authors as the literary giants of their time. And both of them hated, really hated, that time—the twentieth century, from the First through the Second World War—and what they knew was sure to follow it.

They saw in modern life a terrible enemy. It was not only totalitarianism that they loathed but virtually everything that would come even if totalitarianism was defeated. They saw an end to common sense and common purpose. They saw the futility of life without roots or faith. They saw the emptiness of an existence whose only point was material consumption. And in the great work of their lives, which was to warn us of what was to come, they came to be, improbably enough, in many ways the same man.

But that is our story. And it must begin with theirs.

THE SAME MAN

CHAPTER 1

Cutting Class

—

WHEN ERIC BLAIR'S FATHER, RICHARD WALMESLEY Blair, retired from his lifetime work as an imperial civil servant in India, he returned to England and ended his days at a small seaside resort town called Southwold. He was neither rich nor highly educated, nor had his career been marked by anything that might be considered noteworthy. But he was, in his own eyes and in the eyes of Southwold, a man who clearly commanded respect.

Sunday in Southwold was a day of promenade. Nearly everyone in town turned out for a leisurely stroll, but that does not mean that they fraternized. One only greeted, or indeed even acknowledged, others more or less of one's own class—and there were nearly as many gradations of class in Southwold as there were families.

Take, for example, Jack Wilkenson Denny, the leading tailor in town. He had made three-piece suits, flannel trousers, and riding breeches for the Blairs; his cloth and workmanship were of the highest quality.

It was a small town. Richard Blair was a regular customer of Jack Denny. And yet when they passed on the Southwold promenade, "Mr. Blair would walk straight past him without a gesture of recognition," one villager remembered.

This was not the least bit surprising to the slighted Mr. Denny. It was part of the natural order of things. "Old man Blair was truly aristocratic," he said, by way of explaining the snub, "a typical retired civil servant."

And Denny, for his own part, was quick to describe himself as a "high class" tradesman—and therefore entitled to withhold cordiality when passing the village grocer, who in turn could look down on someone else.

It is impossible to exaggerate the power of class distinctions in England in the early years of the twentieth century, when both Evelyn Waugh and Eric Blair were raised. It is difficult today even to *imagine* it. Life was a scoreboard, and each person's score was posted at birth.

Everyone knew who was above or below them in social ranking. Total strangers could be socially slotted within seconds with appalling precision. (Eric Blair, as George Orwell, later wrote that he had been born into "the lower-upper-middle class.") Most people could just *sense* the social standing of anyone they encountered. It is no wonder the English invented radar.

Richard Blair may have seemed aristocratic to his tailor, but he couldn't fool a real aristocrat. His only upper-class connection was to one Charles Blair (1743–1820), Eric's great-great-grandfather, a rich man (sugar and slaves) who had married Mary Fane, the youngest daughter of the eighth Earl of Westmorland. One of their sons was Richard's grandfather. So Richard had only a very distant relationship to the aristocracy. He had a portrait of his ancestress and some monogrammed silver. Nothing more.

The class system was so powerful, though, that those tenuous little threads to a distant noble past, however thinly stretched, remained unbroken and revered. Even after he had transformed himself into George Orwell, Eric kept Mary Fane's portrait with him all his life, transferring it from one squalid dwelling to the next. It was like the light from a dead star, still traveling through time and space.

But one can't live on that. And Richard Blair had to make a living. Jobs at home were scarce, but fortunately for Richard the British had an empire. The imperial civil service was often the only avenue open to men of gentle birth but limited means. It offered respectable careers in exotic lands, but only to those on Richard's rung or higher on the social ladder. Members of the working class did not share in this opportunity. Their sons never rose in the British Empire.

Richard Blair, however, came from a family to which imperial service was not only an option but a godsend, and something of a family tradition. Richard's father had also found work abroad, becoming an Anglican deacon in Calcutta, then a priest in Tasmania, and finally returning home to end his days as a well-paid vicar in Dorset, thanks to the not-quite-unraveled Fane connection.

So Richard went into the family business of occupying imperial sinecures. At the age of eighteen he left England to become a minor official in the Opium Department of the Government of India. He began as an assistant sub-deputy opium agent, third grade, and for three decades slowly moved upward, ending his career as sub-deputy opium agent, first grade. The empire provided him with a wife as well as a career. Ida Limouzin was much younger than Richard. The daughter of a Frenchman and an Englishwoman, she had lived most of her life in Burma, where the Limouzins were long established. She married Richard in India, in 1896.

The Opium Department of the Government of India, despite its unequivocal name, was not really Indian at all. It was run by Englishmen on behalf of their empire, and was in the highly lucrative business of growing poppies and producing the drug in India, where it was illegal, and then selling it to the people of China, millions of whom became hopelessly addicted. The Chinese government tried to block its ports from this insidious trade. It was for moments like this that England had a navy—ships of the fleet sailed out and bombarded forts along the Chinese coast. Thereafter England could export addiction and crime to China with impunity. Since history is written by the winners, this triumph of thuggery is known simply as the Opium War, which could leave the impression that England was trying to stop the Chinese from selling opium to *them*. It is as if Colombians had destroyed all U.S. border facilities and thereafter, without restriction, hooked the American population on cocaine. This was, for wellborn Englishmen, the nineteenth-century version of the global economy.

It was an economy that provided a secure place for Richard Blair. He led a more comfortable life in India than was attainable for him at home, and his friends, like his speech, remained exclusively English. He waited a long time to get married and, despite the plentitude of servants, seemed in no hurry to fill his house with children. It's almost as if he wanted to postpone family life until he was closer to retirement.

The Blairs' first child was Marjorie, and then, on June 25, 1903, at Motihari in Bengal, she was joined by a brother, Eric Arthur Blair. Richard was forty-six when Eric was born, and Ida was twenty-seven.

Eric's birth prompted the family to return to England. A son must be educated at a good school back home, and "home," regardless of how many generations had been spent primarily away from it, was unquestionably England. Richard would remain in India until his retirement, which seems to have been the principal goal of his career. His pension then, at age fifty-five, would be only £438 per year, but that was just enough, if one were careful, to give the right impression. Richard would have spent his entire career in His Majesty's service, quite untainted by "trade" (the poppies didn't count). He would be able to find, as eventually he did, a nice little place to live in the green English countryside and a club where he could golf. The club would be closed to those in trade.

That was all still years away for Richard, but it was thought best not to raise, let alone educate, the children in India—and so Ida Blair took Eric, still an infant, and Marjorie back to England. Richard didn't see any of them for three years, when he went to England for a three-month visit; he then returned to India for four more years until his retirement. (Eric gained another sister nine months after his father's visit.)

So until he was eight, Eric Blair scarcely saw his father. His mother must have been busy, with much less household help than she had enjoyed under the Raj. Eric's health was already cause for some concern. The bronchial problems that would plague him all his life were evident from the start, as was his verbal precocity. His first spoken word was "beastly." Perhaps he picked it up from his mother, complaining about the sudden absence of servants.

But Eric Blair's childhood was not beastly. For a while it was sublime. His early years were golden, a word he later used to describe a longed-for past. (In *1984*, Winston Smith dreams of a "golden country," hazily remembered from his youth.) The Edwardian age was indeed the golden sunset of the country gentry. The Blairs had found a comfortable home in Henley-on-Thames, a market town in a lush river valley in Oxfordshire. In Orwell's memories it was always summer—a world of sunlit green and gold, fishing and fields and games, the smell and buzz of nature soft and near, and, borne by the breeze from the river, the faint lapping sound of oars in water.

It was paradise for a sensitive boy who liked to be left alone. When he did want company there were other children nearby. His lovely mother read to him, and then there was the joy of reading on his own. There was the absence of reproach. He was his mother's favorite. He was loved, he was unthreatened, and he was free. If the Blairs had been richer, nannies would have kept a watchful eye. If poorer, he would be crowded in an urban slum, probably hungry and perhaps already at work. But he was at exactly the right place on the English social scoreboard for a child of five or six or seven—unrestrained in the soft warmth of languorous summer, comforted by the certitudes both of society and of nature, free to explore unguardedly the fertile world outside his door. Beyond Eric's family's hedge were endless fields, fearless adventure, and the simple joy of careless pleasure. Cyril Connolly, who knew him nearly as long as anyone, would say that George Orwell was a radical who was permanently in love with the year 1910. Indeed he was: 1910 was his golden country.

But in the next year his world became a nightmare. The expulsion from Eden was brutal and abrupt.

In 1911, it was time for eight-year-old Eric to go away to school. He had already, with his sisters, attended a local church school during the day, and it had been an extension of the comforts he had known—praise and affection, happy progress, accomplished goals.

However, that wasn't really *school*. School was where you went from the age of twelve until eighteen. After that, you could go to university—Oxford or Cambridge—or into a military college, the military directly, or the service, which administered the empire. Or you could just lead the local hunt three days a week.

But whatever you did was not as important as where you had attended school. Of all the questions meant to find and put you in your place, the sharpest by far was "Where did you go to school?"

The best answer—for many families the only conceivable answer—was Eton. There were other schools, of course, Harrow, Rugby, Westminster, and so on. These were fine, too, especially if they were a family tradition. All of them were private and, of course, expensive. In Britain, they are called "public" schools, and in Eric Blair's day they were the most integral part of the English class system. And the apogee of that system was, without any question, Eton.

Eton was so high that you had to attain other summits first, private preparatory schools that then became launching pads. They prepared you to get into "school," which was Eton and its respectable alternatives.

The word "meritocracy" had not yet been coined, because there was nothing for it to describe. Even the word "intelligent" was applied with some restraint back then. A student gifted in his studies was instead called "clever." Monkeys were clever, too. But sometimes clever boys were needed to help run the empire, and if there were not enough of them at the best schools already, others had to be recruited.

None of this applied to families of ancient title or great wealth, many of whose sons were enrolled in Eton at birth. The preparatory schools were there to fill the spaces that remained. That's why they mattered so.

Most of them were boarding schools. Each was a world unto itself, its rules absolute. The most prestigious prep schools, like the public schools, preferred lineage to ability, but they also needed to send some students on to Eton through their stellar performances in its entrance exam. This would suggest a high level of instruction and therefore attract the sons of the newly rich who couldn't take Eton for granted on family name alone.

Eric Blair was just such a clever little boy. His family wanted to make the most of that, so they sent him to a preparatory school called St. Cyprian's, in Sussex. This required some sacrifice on their part. Tuition at St. Cyprian's was £180 per year, more than 40 percent of Richard Blair's retirement income. But Eric Blair was a *very* clever little boy, as his local teachers had recognized, and St. Cyprian's knew that his academic success would burnish the school's reputation. So they admitted him at the discounted rate of £90 per year—still a stretch for the Blairs, but they managed to find it.

Eric may have been admitted to St. Cyprian's, but he was never welcome there. He was regarded as a necessary encumbrance, a costly and unattractive investment in academic reputation. Right from the start, the headmaster and his wife displayed a cruelty that never abated and made no effort to conceal the cold disdain with which he was regarded. His classmates were no better. He needed no reminders of his lowly status, but even so they were incessant. Eric's school life was a living hell.

We know this from Eric Blair's own pen, but it took a lifetime before he was able to pour out his pain. Shortly before his death, George Orwell finally wrote an account of his years at St. Cyprian's. He called it, sardonically, "Such, Such Were the

Joys." It is as powerful as anything he ever wrote, and painful to read. It couldn't be published in England until 1968, when the widow of the headmaster finally died, ending the possibility of action for libel.

Forty years had passed since Eric Blair's torture. Forty years, and every wound was still fresh. With cool lucidity, in fifteen thousand words, a chronicle of torment proceeds, and it is a cry from the heart—the harsh portrait of a helpless and continual victim of sadism and snobbery.

The headmaster and his wife set the tone. They humiliated Eric constantly. He was beaten and publicly ridiculed for wetting his bed. He was the only boy denied a cake to share with the others on his birthday, presumably because his family was paying reduced fees.

Blair's financial status may not have been responsible for these outrages, but he clearly *felt* they were. He wrote that he doubted that the son of a family with an income over £2,000 a year would be beaten as he had been. We don't know. The disgusting filth and smells and the ghastly food of the place, if accurately described, must have been shared by all the boys equally. Some of them would write in response to "Such, Such Were the Joys" that its account was exaggerated and unfair. Perhaps. Eric was not the kind of boy who easily adapts to boarding school. He had been raised in an entirely feminine home where he had known strong maternal love and a life without harshness. Sensitive and gentle, he had been plucked overnight from one kind of world and consigned to its opposite. True, others may have seen that world differently. But there is no question of how Blair saw it or how the experience forged George Orwell.

Almost all of his classmates were from families better off

than his, and the custom at that time was to let him know it. Soon enough he knew precisely where he stood. "In a world where the prime necessities were money, titled relatives, athleticism, tailor-made clothes, neatly brushed hair, a charming smile, I was no good."

For Eric Blair, the worst thing about the school was that it was a rehearsal for the real world—"a continuous triumph of the strong over the weak. Virtue consisted in winning: it consisted in being bigger, stronger, handsomer, richer, more popular, more elegant, more unscrupulous than other people—in dominating them, bullying them." It was the system, he concluded, and his thoughts became political. He wanted to change the system in which a sensitive boy was bullied by students and teachers alike because his father made no more than £400 per year.

The students knew each classmate's family income. They knew because they asked: "How much do you have?" By this they did not mean "How much does your family earn?" It meant "How much does your family receive each year?" To "earn" money somehow tainted it. It implied that one had to *work* for a living. Some people did, of course, and if they earned *enough*—a great deal—then it was all right. But the best thing was just to "have" your money. The original fortune may have come from land, the sale of opium or slaves, or from any enterprise—shipping, cotton mills, or coal mines, if they were out of sight and not managed by the owners. But the best of all was wealth from land. Rich stockbrokers bought country estates to imply that their wealth was from land. Their grandchildren believed it. A minister with good family contacts would be given a "living" along with his assignment to a fashionable pulpit, which meant an annual income rooted in rent from the parish. After Blair became Orwell, he referred to this class as *rentiers,* the French socialist term for those subsidized over generations by the income from land they themselves did not work.

New boys were immediately questioned by bigger boys about their place in the permanent order.

"How much a year has your pater got? What part of London do you live in? Is that Knightsbridge or Kensington? How many bathrooms has your house got? How many servants do your people keep? Have you got a butler? Well, then, have you got a cook? Where do you get your clothes made?" Blair remembered every question, exactly as it had been asked.

Since his own answers were clearly inadequate, Blair concluded:

> I was no good, and could not be any good. . . . It was not only money that mattered: there were also strength, beauty, charm, athleticism and something called "guts" or "character," which in reality was the power to impose your will on others. I did not possess any of those qualities. . . . I had no money, I was weak, I was ugly, I was unpopular, I had a chronic cough, I was cowardly, I smelt. . . .
>
> The conviction that it was *not possible* for me to be a success went deep enough to influence my actions til far into adult life. Until I was about thirty I always planned my life on the assumption . . . that any major undertaking was bound to fail.

To young Blair the most painful of all class distinctions stemmed from the school's "curious cult of Scotland." In Orwell's essay, the taunts over Scotland seem the cruelest of all.

The real reason for the cult of Scotland was that only very rich people could spend their summers there. . . . Scotland was a private paradise which a few initiates could talk about and make outsiders feel small.

"You going to Scotland this hols?"

"Rather! We go every year."

"My pater's got three miles of river."

"My pater's giving me a new gun for the twelfth. There's jolly good black game where we go. Get out [Blair]! What are you listening for? You've never been in Scotland. I bet you don't know what a blackcock looks like!"

Eric Blair did not belong, and this shocked him. He hadn't known this before. There had been the portrait of Mary Fane, a crest on their silver, a father who had gone out to serve the empire—but now all of a sudden Eric was the lowest of the low. In the world of St. Cyprian's, you had to have either a title or money, and of course the Blairs had neither. Their memories didn't matter. The thread was broken.

Eric Blair did keep his part of the bargain with St. Cyprian's. He was admitted to Eton, which was a coup for his headmasters. It should have pleased the fourteen-year-old Eric as well; as a King's Scholar, he was charged virtually no tuition at the most prestigious school in the land. There was no better entrée to the two great universities, Oxford or Cambridge, or to acquaintanceship and then friendship with the nation's future leaders in every field. It was the best of all keys to success.

But he didn't turn that key. It wasn't only that he had lost the confidence to succeed—he did not want success. Not that kind, as defined by a society he loathed. He would not affirm these standards by achieving them. So he chose to fail in the eyes of his enemies. He did little work at Eton. He made few friends. He got poor grades. Even so, he might have achieved a full scholarship to Oxford or Cambridge but did not bother to seek it. The bullies at St. Cyprian's had taught him that even with an Oxford degree he could never succeed in life.

So Eton was as far as his education would go. He stood back from the springboard and looked for another pool. At nineteen, Eric Blair joined the Indian Imperial Police and asked to be sent to Burma.

EVELYN ARTHUR ST. JOHN WAUGH was born in 1903, only a few months after Eric Blair. There any similarity might seem to end.

To begin, Waugh did not have an absent father. Quite the contrary. His father, Arthur Waugh, was impossible to miss. He was a natural actor whose family became his audience.

But he did have his favorites in the audience. There seems to be little doubt that his focus was on his first son, Alec, five years senior to Evelyn. Alec was a natural athlete and his father, who was not, compensated for his own failing through his zeal as a spectator at Alec's games. This did not escape Evelyn's notice. (Nothing ever did.)

"Daddy loves Alec more than me but you love me more than you love Alec," Evelyn said to his mother, hoping for assent.

He received a mother's answer: "No, I love you both the same."

"Then I am lacking in love," said Evelyn.

He was not lacking in class consciousness. When his nurse,

Lucy, scolded little Evelyn and a friend, he complained, "Lucy has no business to speak to us like that."

"Why?" asked the friend.

"Because we're of a much better class than she is."

Evelyn *was* in a better class than Lucy, but how did he stack up with little Eric Blair? They ranked about the same, even though the Waughs were better educated and made more money. The English class system was tricky in this regard. Arthur Waugh was an Oxford graduate. He wrote poetry. He loved literature. After rejecting on practical grounds the stage career for which nature clearly had intended him, he became a publisher. And a very prominent one. He was the managing director of Chapman & Hall, the publishers of Carlyle, Trollope, Thackeray, Dickens, and later Wells and Maugham. He also reviewed books regularly for the *Daily Telegraph*, and was very well paid for doing so.

But he probably couldn't have been admitted to Arthur Blair's club in Southwold. It would have had to be determined first whether a publisher was "in trade"—a question worthy of Talmudic scholars, none of whom, rest assured, would have been consulted.

Arthur Waugh came from Scottish stock, as did his wife, Catherine Charlotte Raban. Her great-great-grandfather was Henry, Lord Cockburn, a distinguished Scots judge. Many of Arthur's ancestors had been in the professions, primarily medicine and the church. One was the pharmacist to Queen Victoria. Catherine's family had been tradesmen and merchants and eventually had careers in the army and the Indian Civil Service. By the early 1800s they had prospered enough to have been granted a coat of arms.

Arthur's father, Alexander Waugh, was a gifted and successful doctor who displayed many of the traits that were to become notoriously associated with his grandson Evelyn. He is often seen as the tree that the apple fell not far from. Alexander Waugh's nickname was "the Brute." His family suffered from his sudden outbreaks of fierce rage and from treatment often disgustingly cruel. (Upon being taught the meaning of the word "sadist," Arthur exclaimed, "Ah, that is what my father must have been.") The Brute would place his small son on a very high tree branch and leave him there for hours before announcing his return by firing a shotgun closely behind the boy's ear. When he saw that a wasp was on his wife's forehead, he struck it with the ivory top of his cane. He made his son kiss the rifles in his gun case. Dr. Waugh loved the theater, and anyone not knowing his real profession would have thought him an actor. In a sense, of course, he was, declaiming scenes from Shakespeare and regarding, as would his son and grandson, his whole life as one long performance, with no intermissions.

Arthur Waugh made over £600 a year with Chapman & Hall, and the same again as a reviewer. This was very much more than Richard Blair received, but the Blair income was fixed and Waugh's subject to changes in the marketplace.

Both families had modest bragging rights on ancestors. The Waughs had a number of successful professionals, though no earl, in the distant past. Still, there was that coat of arms, which, though not really granted to his branch of the family, was later placed by Evelyn above the doorway of his house.

If Orwell claimed to be a member of the "lower-upper-middle class," then where would Waugh have placed his own origins? His life provides the answer: He would have denied them altogether. His presence on the board of the Southwold club would not have guaranteed his father's admission. (He felt that publishers were in trade, though apparently believed that authors were not.)

To say that Evelyn Waugh was a social climber is to describe Everest as a hill. One incident alone establishes the degree of his obsession. The Waughs lived in a respectably ugly detached house in a leafy neighborhood near London. When they chose the place to build their house, they could easily imagine they were moving to the country. Their address was simply North End Road, a quiet country lane between the villages of Hampstead and Golders Green. But then the London tube sent out its tentacles, and before long Golders Green was transformed from a village to a suburb, one almost quintessentially middle-class. Hampstead, however, still had its heath, whose pastoral charms had been captured by two of its former residents, Keats and Constable. The social difference between the two places was considerable. With the growth in population it was no longer possible to list a street name and number as one's sole address; a neighborhood or town was needed, too. So while the Waughs may have continued to occupy a home they named Underhill at 145 North End Road, to the post office they now lived in Golders Green. Evelyn was so ashamed of this that when home on vacation from Oxford he would walk all the way to Hampstead in order to mail letters to his university friends, thus acquiring a false but more fashionable postmark. Neither rain nor sleet nor hail could lure him to post his correspondence nearer to home.

The class system absolutely stamped the lives of Orwell and Waugh from early childhood. In Orwell's case he rejected the system completely and chose not to compete on its terms. His entire life was consistent with this resolve. Waugh embraced the system as it was and devoted his life to rising within it to the very top.

Why did they react in opposite ways to the same rigid social code? Orwell answered for himself in "Such, Such Were the Joys." One cannot read that essay without knowing that it meant as much to him as the book he was also working on at the time, *1984*. The torments of school not only drove him to spend his life among the oppressed but also fueled his lifetime battle against the dictators who bullied entire populations. If anyone tore down the Berlin wall, George Orwell did.

School forged Waugh's life as well, but while Blair was a victim of his classmates, Waugh, a first-rate schoolyard bully, was adroit at victimizing others.

There were other factors, too. Aside from the fact that they were very different sorts of people (Waugh was, after all, descended from "the Brute"), the circumstances of their schooling were also not the same.

And this may have made the critical difference. Waugh was not sent away to boarding school until relatively late in the game. All the years that Blair was suffering at St. Cyprian's, Waugh was living with his parents and going to a school only a twenty-minute walk away. In his first year, he even came home for lunch.

When he was enrolled in nearby Heath Mount at the age of seven, the plan was for him to stay there for only a few years and then move on to prep school, which of course would be a boarding school far from home.

But when he was eleven, the First World War began. It would change everything in England, for everyone, and to a degree unimaginable in 1914. The effect of the war on Arthur Waugh was immediate. His income fell dramatically, by more than half, because his reviewing work was canceled—the daily papers now had other things to print. And a number of Chapman & Hall's writers, as well as staff, were going off to war, so fewer books were being produced.

The Waughs could no longer afford a housemaid, and she was let go. But that was not enough. Arthur simply didn't have the money to send Evelyn to boarding school, so the boy remained at Heath Mount, close to home. He did not face the rigors, discipline, and dislocation of boarding school until he was much older and better able to withstand them. And being able to go home each night meant that school was not his only world. His early school days, therefore, were comfortable and happy.

His happiness included the opportunity to bully other boys. This was in his blood, and the addition of an astonishingly fertile imagination, plus an apparent absence of fear, allowed him to terrorize many of his classmates, regardless of their size. Evelyn shoved other boys around, won fistfights, gave out highly creative and deeply offensive nicknames, and attracted a pack of like-minded brutes to run to ground the meek and innocent.

And as life, Waugh's only comic rival, would have it, one of Evelyn's classmates at Heath Mount was little Cecil Beaton. The man who would do the sets for *My Fair Lady* was then "a beautiful boy with blond hair, thick eyelashes and an unforgivably girlish demeanor." For Beaton, Heath Mount should have been much less threatening than a boarding school, but then, as from a darkening sky, fell Evelyn Waugh. Beaton never got over the physical pain (including being stuck with pins) and verbal abuse the bully delivered to him. Suffice to say that many years later, successful and supposedly secure, Beaton wrote to a friend, "Evelyn is a very sinister character, & I have been secretly frightened of him ever since my first morning at my first

school when he came up in the 'break' & started to bully me."
The two met often at Mayfair parties in the 1930s, and Beaton
tried to stay on his own side of the room.

Their relationship at school recalls an observation by the
author Tom Wolfe, on why some people become liberals and
others conservatives. Wolfe said that the bullies in school grew
up to be conservatives and the kids they picked on became liberals. Whether or not this rule is universal, it seems to have
been the case with Orwell and Waugh.

But all good things must come to an end, and Waugh finally
had to exchange the joys of blood sports for new-boy status at a
boarding school. It was 1917 and he was nearly fourteen. If he
didn't go to a prep school soon his chances of getting into a
good university would be slim. So his father, however financially pinched, sent him to Lancing (exactly the absurd but
somehow apt sort of name that Waugh the writer would give a
boarding school), a cold, gray monastic place in Sussex, near
Brighton.

Lancing was Waugh's Eton. It was not remotely as prestigious a place, but Waugh took care of that in later years by portraying it in his short stories, quite falsely, as an aristocratic
enclave whose students spoke of grouse moors and Scotland [!]
and who stayed at Claridge's when on break. Lancing was, in
point of fact, quite a religious school, and many of its students
were the sons of clergymen.

The fastidious Waugh was as appalled at the lack of privacy,
the bad food, and the physical discomforts of boarding school
as Blair had been. But he didn't *hate* Lancing as the other
schoolboy hated St. Cyprian's. For one thing, he was older, and
he was able to fit in. There is always room for another bully in
a boarding school, and Waugh was always witty, charming

when he chose to be, and preternaturally gifted at making friends.

There was something else as well. At Lancing, Waugh was seen as a financially privileged student. His father had entered him in Head's House, whose headmaster was also the head of school, making it the place to be for those who cared about such things, which was everyone—and Evelyn most of all. This privilege cost Arthur Waugh only £10 a year extra, which he was able to find, but of course it made all the difference. Evelyn was in the in crowd, which, however affordable its attainment, simulated the money rankings that dominated loftier boarding schools.

Thus, though his father lacked the money to send him to boarding school until late in the game, once there Evelyn assumed a sense of social superiority. Waugh was not exactly *popular* at Lancing, but he was a success. Indeed, unlike Blair, he was learning that success in life was possible. He was house captain, editor of the school magazine, and president of the Debating Society. A good student, he set his sights on Oxford. He had visited there and told his diary, "I have never seen anything so beautiful." Since there was no chance of his attending Oxford without a scholarship, Waugh studied with great diligence for the exam.

Those were not the days of multiple-choice examinations. Instead, the students in the Oxford exam room were required to write a series of essays. In Waugh's case, this was like handing Vermeer a brush. Soon he was notified that he had won the Hertford history scholarship, worth £100 a year, enough to ensure his attendance. He also received a letter of congratulations from the dean of Hertford College, C.R.M.F. Cruttwell, who said that he had found "the quality of your English style about the best of any of the candidates in the group." The name "Cruttwell" was no doubt new to Waugh back then. His letter must have been a source of warmth and good feeling. That was to change. Poor Cruttwell could not know the danger that was coming his way.

CHAPTER 2

At the Bottom of the Hill

—

WHEN EVELYN WAUGH ARRIVED AT OXFORD IN JAN-
uary 1922, he looked around and feared it was already too late
for him to really belong, because he hadn't been to Eton. All his
uncanny social-climbing instincts told him at once that "Oxford" was a mere abstraction, and that the place was in fact a
constellation of clubs.

And of these the best was Eton. It must have seemed to
Waugh that each Eton class was accepted in its entirety by the
university. This was not quite so. Some Etonians actually went
to Cambridge, and there were even cases where they didn't go
on to university at all. (Eric Blair, for example, was on a boat to
Burma.) But, by and large, there was a sizable contingent of
scholars, aesthetes, and peers who knew one another from Eton
and maintained their previous associations at Oxford. There
was nothing formal about it, no incorporation, nor stationery,
nor meeting place, but Waugh knew a club when he saw one,
and the Old Etonians group was impossible to miss.

It certainly had colorful members, even for Oxford. One of
these was Edward James, who lived in the most extravagant
suite of rooms in college and who was widely believed to be the
illegitimate son of King Edward VII. One well-regarded biographer of Waugh and his circle concludes that Edward James

"may have been not only the King's son, but also his grandson," and offers circumstantial evidence to support this. Edward James became a major patron of surrealism and eventually moved to Mexico to raise orchids.

And he wasn't even the most flamboyant Etonian at Oxford. That distinction was nailed down by Brian Howard—immortally, as he was the primary model for Anthony Blanche in *Brideshead Revisited*. Openly homosexual, he was described by Waugh, quoting Lady Caroline Lamb on Lord Byron, as "mad, bad and dangerous to know." A literary gadfly and reviewer, he would eventually die by suicide.

It is astonishing how many future lights of English letters not only were at Oxford with Waugh but had been together at Eton before that.

There was, for example, Harold Acton, "the dominant undergraduate aesthete of his Oxford generation" and a lifelong friend of Waugh's. He was born at, and later inherited, a famous and opulent villa outside Florence, La Pietra. (No wonder Waugh didn't want his letters postmarked from Golders Green.) Acton wrote a number of books, enlivened and influenced the London literary scene, and was eventually knighted. It was thought that he would dominate English letters.

So many of the Etonians seemed headed for success. If you had asked Waugh's Oxford classmates who among them was most likely to become a famous author, the preponderant choice probably would have been Cyril Connolly, "the cleverest boy of his generation," with Harold Acton the runner-up. Connolly had been at St. Cyprian's and Eton with Eric Blair and was now at Oxford with Waugh. He would be helpful to each in his career as an editor and reviewer. He was a novelist as well, though never even remotely reaching the heights of his two early classmates. In 1950, he was commissioned to write a profile on Waugh for *Time*, but it was never published. When he died, in 1974, his obituary in *The Times* noted, "As he himself well knew, he never fully lived up to his gifts."

Another Etonian, Anthony Powell, was an Oxford classmate who did become a major writer. His *Dance to the Music of Time* sequence of twelve novels is important both as literature and as a portrait of its period. He was one of Waugh's favorite authors.

And Henry Yorke, the son of a Birmingham businessman and relative of the Earls of Hardwicke, actually published his first novel when he and Waugh were still at Oxford. His subsequent novels were published under the pseudonym Henry Green, and, quite unusually for that time and his background, dealt primarily with the lives of working-class people.

From all these names one might suppose that most Etonians at Oxford were aesthetes or writers. This was very much not so. Most were far more enthralled with sports and London dances and planning their futures than with poems that didn't rhyme. Those who went on too much about the arts were often scorned and sometimes dunked in the college fountain pool.

But the relative unpopularity of the aesthetes made them more accessible to Waugh. In *Brideshead*, Charles Ryder's cousin bemoans the fact that Charles at Oxford has "gone straight hook, line and sinker, into *the very worst set in the university.*" He can't understand it. But Waugh, unlike his fictional character, was not operating on romantic whim. He was making the friends that he could. He saw the special place that Eton had at Oxford—indeed, in England—and since he hadn't been to Eton, the best he could do was befriend those who had. And since most of them had no interest in befriending him, he had to find those who did. This, as it turned out, was the group that had been active together in the Eton Society of Arts.

Waugh was in Hertford College, one of the least fashionable. (At Oxford, even the colleges were like clubs.) His only friends at first were those he'd known at Lancing, from families not so different from his own. And then he met Harold Acton. He'd never met anyone like him before. (If only he'd given Beaton half a chance.) Through him, Waugh met the others from Acton's set at Eton, who soon became his friends, too.

What they first saw in Waugh was an incomparable wit. He also had an unstoppable drive that none of them possessed, and though less tutored in the great world than they were, was swiftly catching up by using them as his text. They saw him as ebullient, bold, and unpredictable, the embodiment of their first commandment, which was never to be boring.

What he saw in them was freedom. These people were free to do whatever they wanted. They knew no constraints. Not money, not class, not rules—no fetters at all on their youthful zest. They could live solely for beauty and pleasure. They were different from other people. You could see it in the way they stood, the way they spoke—the *languor* of those Etonians. They owned the world. You couldn't miss it. (Even Orwell, pretending to be a tramp, needed only to cross a room and speak; the moment one heard his accent the jig was up: He'd been to Eton. John le Carré, many years later, wrote, "I taught at Eton. It always amused me that Blair-Orwell, who had been to Eton, took great pains to disown the place, while Evelyn Waugh, who hadn't been to Eton, took similar pains to pretend he had.")

It was all very well to be in with at least some of the Eton crowd, but that wasn't quite enough. At Oxford you had to join a *real* club, too. Among other things, a club was the only place in which an undergraduate could get convivially drunk. Oxford forbade its students to drink in the local village pubs, so students eagerly sought out clubs with their own bars. Even Etonians needed one.

Some clubs were very grand and restricted largely to those of noble birth. Of these, the Bullingdon was the most exclusive. Many of its members were Etonians, though none of Waugh's new crowd. When the Bullingdon assembled for dinner its members were hard to miss. The club uniform was white tie and tails, but the tailcoats were bright green, and, so clad, the young lords were wont to end an evening of excessive drink by rampaging through the campus to physically harass the hapless scholars who crossed their path. It was much like the hunts they enjoyed back home, only with aesthetes like Acton as the fox.

Though Waugh would gladly have led its pack, the Bullingdon was closed inalterably even to considering him for membership. But there were many other clubs at Oxford. When Waugh first arrived he joined what was then one of the least fashionable, which had two large rooms and a bar over a bicycle shop. This was called the Hypocrites Club. Its motto, in Greek, was perfect: "Water is best." A lot of drinking went on at the Hypocrites, mostly after Waugh joined, as he was soon followed by his new pals, who proceeded to completely transform the place. The discussions of philosophy that had formerly made up the principal entertainment were supplanted by drunken and licentious revels. To stand out at Oxford then as dissipated took some doing, but they did it. Some of the members of the Hypocrites, of whom Brian Howard was the archetype, were certainly gay, though probably most were not. There was enough dalliance on that side of the fence to require a notice on the club wall warning that "gentlemen may prance but not dance." The rule was not always obeyed. Waugh certainly had some romantic, though perhaps not physical, attachments with classmates at Oxford.

It's a wonder he found the time, since it meant taking his foot off the rail of the bar. Waugh's lifetime of excessive drink began at the Hypocrites Club. There he did not drink alone. Much of the Eton group seemed lured to the perpetual party. The Oxford authorities began to take notice of this crowd when one of the Hypocrites, Lord Clonmore, gave a supper party on the roof of a church. The club had maintained a semblance of respectability by electing as its president Lord Elmley, scion of the Lygon family, whose members became the models for the aristocratic Marchmains in *Brideshead Revisited*. Any stature gained by the Hypocrites through the selection of Elmley was more than offset by the drunken majority vote for Waugh as secretary. No minutes were ever taken.

The Hypocrites Club was shut down by the devotedly Catholic dean of Balliol College after an infamous fancy dress party that included members dressed as nuns and choirboys with vermilion lips.

The closure of his favorite bar did not drive Waugh back to his studies. There were other clubs and other parties. The Oxford Railway Club had just been founded by John Sutro, who would remain a close friend throughout Waugh's life, and whose own outsider status (he was Jewish) had not kept him from Oxford's inner circle. The Oxford Railway Club included Lord Rosse, Hugh Lygon, Harold Acton, Bryan Guinness, Patrick Balfour, Henry Yorke, Roy Harrod, Lord Weymouth, David Plunket Greene, Lord Stavordale, Brian Howard, and Evelyn Waugh. The members would enjoy a black-tie dinner on the Penzance–Aberdeen express between Oxford and Leicester, and then would take a return train from Leicester to Oxford, that leg of the journey devoted to speeches and after-dinner drinks.

Since the point of Oxford for Waugh was getting to know as many people as possible, he joined clubs indiscriminately, without regard for their purpose. So he joined the Carlton, which was politically conservative, and the New Reform, whose members were liberal. He even joined the White Rose, a dining club devoted to promoting the Stuart claim to the British throne. He drew caricatures for the school paper and he ran for the Oxford Union, the elite debating society that attracted aspiring prime ministers. He did everything he could at Oxford except open a book or attend a class. He did not, however, join any of the dramatic societies, "preferring," in the words of a friend, "to confine his acting to private life."

The neglect of his studies came early to the attention of the dean of his college, C.R.M.F. Cruttwell, the same man who had so hopefully welcomed Waugh to Oxford.

Cruttwell was not merely the dean, he was also Waugh's tutor. This was an unfortunate pairing—for both of them, as it turned out. Cruttwell was a serious scholar and in some pain from a wartime leg wound. He liked to intimidate his charges. When Waugh translated the Latin verb *eramus* as "Erasmus," Cruttwell snapped, "Damn you, you're a scholar. If you can't show industry, I at least have the right to expect intelligence." Waugh was stunned.

When provoked, Waugh's usual response was both savagely harsh and remarkably inventive. And he was very easily provoked. There are two meanings to the word "sensitive": "highly perceptive" and "easily hurt." In human nature these tend to be a package deal, and in both meanings of the word Waugh was astonishingly sensitive.

And so, when Cruttwell finally called Waugh "a silly suburban sod with an inferiority complex," a major war began. No words could have wounded him more. The fanciful balloon of upper-class inclusion had been punctured, and its occupant dropped back into Golders Green. Cruttwell did not know what he had started. There are worse fates than being shot in the leg.

Waugh waited patiently for vengeance worthy of the slight. One day in a lecture Cruttwell remarked, "Of course a dog cannot have rights." It was a casual illustration of a philosophical point.

But it was enough for Waugh. He said to a classmate that Cruttwell's remark was that of someone who obviously wanted to violate the animal sexually. In fact, Waugh continued, his improvised seedling already sprouting wildly, the dean probably does this shameful thing on a regular basis. Of course he says dogs have no rights!

Waugh then proceeded to widely circulate elaborate fantasies concerning Cruttwell's sexual relations with dogs. He composed some (there is no other word for it) doggerel on this subject and drunkenly shouted the verses across the quad. He bought a stuffed dog with the announced intent of entrapping Cruttwell for all to see. He went so far as to bark outside the dean's windows at night in order to lend credence to the slurs.

It didn't end there. For Waugh, it never really ended. In many of the works he would write in future years—*Decline and Fall, Black Mischief, Scoop, A Handful of Dust*—a repulsive or ridiculous character is named Cruttwell. The poor dean would die in an insane asylum.

Why did a small dart launch a lifetime of counterattack? Because the dart had hit home. Waugh had been hit in his most vulnerable spot, his middle-class origins, and his response was not merely to launch a full strike against Cruttwell, but to redouble his efforts to prove, especially to himself, that his proper place on the social ladder was at the top.

Waugh's time at Oxford was devoted to pleasure. And rising ominously just beyond it was debt. He was now running with a very rich crowd. Not all, but many of his new friends had enormous wealth to spend, and it was easy to see how they spent it. Some brought several horses with them when they came to Oxford, to alternate mounts for their daily ride. Some spent thousands of pounds a year at school, quite apart from tuition and housing, primarily on clothes and entertainment—this at a time when the average income of British doctors was less than £400 a year. The very highest level of the English aristocracy was much less well off after the Great War, because the war had bankrupted Britain, and they owned Britain. But theirs was a last hurrah; many who held titles still were rich, and those who no longer were did not seem to know it. So Oxford, even in Waugh's time, was a place of languid privilege. All students, regardless of wealth, were waited on by servants. The better-off vied with one another over the vintages to serve at sumptuous luncheon parties that lasted until dusk.

This was the garden of earthly delights in which Waugh now foraged. The tight bud of his lavish nature flowered mightily, vivid and pungent. Horses, of course, were out of the question, but not the latest clothes. The standard of male raiment at Oxford was very high: Charvet ties and dressing gowns, shirts of silk and crepe de chine, bespoke suits and hunting jackets and boots as soft as skin, bright scarves for motoring to London, bowlers and hats lined with fur. There was scarcely an item that could be worn to an office or to church. That was the point.

So was expense. All this fine plumage was very costly, which was part of its appeal. Waugh was on a tight allowance from home. Nonetheless, in matters sartorial he competed quite effectively, for London tailors routinely extended credit to Oxford undergraduates. And in the happy time before that particular guillotine fell, Waugh's innate sense of style was first proclaimed by his wardrobe, which drew approving glances from the titled peacocks strutting past. Fundamentally, Waugh's days at Oxford were spent understudying the role he would master in later life.

In truth, the Oxford of indolent luxury did not exist for many undergraduates even then, but thanks to Waugh it is the picture that will most endure. His Oxford became the Oxford of those who had not been there, and it remains a golden place forever through his loving evocation of it. When he sat down to write *Brideshead Revisited* during the Second World War, he tried to make it in part a chronicle of paradise lost, a record of the soft, rich days before austerity and danger had befallen England. The brightest symbol of extravagant freedom was Oxford in the twenties, for the lucky few a life as smooth and sparkling as the river currents on which they punted. "It seemed as if I was being given a brief spell of what I had never known, a happy childhood, and though its toys were silk shirts and liqueurs and cigars and its naughtiness high in the catalogue of grave sins, there was something of nursery freshness about us that fell little short of the joy of innocence," Charles Ryder tells us in *Brideshead Revisited*.

So many great writers have tried to capture Oxford, but Waugh's picture is the one that endured. "Alone among the hundreds of personas that clutter the ancient universities, and are best discarded on leaving, along with the gown and the bicycle clips, Waugh's had a universal resonance, proving not only exactly right for its time and place, but for every time and place since," wrote Wilfrid Sheed in *The New York Review of Books* in 1993.

Since his description of the place will live forever, the least Oxford could have done in return was award him a degree, but that was not to be. There were limits even then to the tolerance of truancy. And he had not exactly endeared himself to Cruttwell, who wrote him a scathing letter discontinuing his scholarship, adding, "I cannot say that your third does you anything but discredit."

Third was indeed a lowly status. The very best students got firsts. Some less able grinds graduated with seconds. A third was not quite the bottom of the barrel; one also could graduate with a fourth, though few did, and indeed it is difficult to imagine greater inattention to the curriculum than Waugh's. Graduating with a third would have been bad enough.

But Waugh did not graduate at all. He needed one more term to qualify for graduation. Recognizing that a diploma with a third would do little to advance his career, and perhaps feeling guilty about asking his father for more tuition money, when it came time for that final term, he simply chose not to go back.

It was 1924, and he was twenty-one years old. Among the peers with whom he'd frolicked, the lack of a degree was almost an honor, a source of hilarity in the distant future when one would warn one's own son, the future earl, to be more studious. But Waugh was not a future earl. He did not appear to be a future anything. He had no degree, no fortune, and no prospects.

His tolerant father paid off his debts, and Evelyn sold some of his costly *objets* to the same end. But he still couldn't afford an apartment of his own, and so once again he was waking up in Golders Green.

The only career that seemed open to him was teaching school. Even then, the first-rate schools, and the second-rate as well, were not interested in instructors with his tarnished academic credentials. So he took what he could get, which was teaching classics at a school in Wales, where the only credential required for employment was that he own a dinner jacket. For the lowly salary of £160 per year, he taught Latin, Greek, and history to the scruffy boys of Arnold House, a public school in Llanddulas in North Wales. It was about as far from what Waugh considered civilization as one could get in the British Isles. The landscape was bleak, the students sullen and unpromising, and the tedium of his duties relieved only by drinking in the local pubs, where only Welsh was spoken. There was the sad escape of traveling back to Oxford when he could, and imbibing with his former classmates. These brief flights to paradise only deepened his despair upon returning to Wales. The Arnold House was made slightly less boring through the addition to its faculty of a flagrant serial pederast.

Waugh knew he had reached rock bottom. Desperate, he sought a job in Italy, but it fell through. He tried to write a novel, but then sent his draft to Acton, who mocked it; this so discouraged Waugh that he threw the manuscript into the Arnold House furnace.

Morbidly, he compared his dismal fate to the happy careers

just beginning for so many of his friends. With no avenue of escape apparent to him, Waugh decided to kill himself. He leaves an account in the memoir of his youth, *A Little Learning*.

> One night, . . . I went down alone to the beach with my thoughts full of death. I took off my clothes and began swimming out to sea. . . . I left a note with my clothes, the quotation from Euripides about the sea which washes away all human ills. I went to the trouble of verifying it, accents and all, from the school text:
>
> Θάλασσα χλύζει πάντα Τ'ανθρώπων χαχά
>
> It was a beautiful night of a gibbous moon. I swam slowly, but before I reached the point of no return [I] was disturbed by a smart on the shoulder. I had run into a jelly-fish. A few more strokes, a second more painful sting. The placid waters were full of the creatures. . . .
>
> I turned about, swam back to the sands. . . . With some difficulty I dressed and tore into small pieces my pretentious classical tag, leaving them to the sea. . . .
>
> Then I climbed the sharp hill that led to all the years ahead.

WHILE WAUGH AND HIS OXFORD friends were drunkenly singing "The Road to Mandalay," Eric Blair had been hard at work patrolling it. This city in upper Burma was his first assignment, the place where he would be trained for his job as an imperial policeman.

He was an officer of the Indian Imperial Police, and, of course, Burma is not in India. The two countries are not even adjacent except at their northern extremities in the Himalayas.

But to the English this didn't matter. Burma was administered as a province of India, and that was that. Buddhist and Asian, it had much more in common with its true neighbor, Siam (later Thailand), but while Siam was an independent kingdom, the British had taken over Burma by force, so now they could choose to consider it part of India, too. The fact that the Burmese had their own religion, language, culture, physiognomy, and history, not to mention country, was beside the point. The point was Administration.

Blair was well aware of the differences between Burma and India. His mother's family, the Limouzins—he called them "the automobiles"—had lived in Burma for generations as teak merchants and shipbuilders. His grandmother still lived there. The Limouzins were Europeans and so were all their friends. The lives they had chosen to live were isolated and far from home, but the ubiquity of servants seemed to make this bearable.

This family connection may explain why Blair requested Burma as his first assignment. His wish was hastily granted. Few of the police candidates actually *wanted* to go to Burma. The action—opportunity for advancement and propinquity to clubs—was in India. Burma was considered a backwater and one with the largest mosquitoes in the empire. The young policeman didn't seem to care. Even at the outset of his career, Blair would regard the smart move as a disincentive.

He was just nineteen. He had had to wait until that birthday to be eligible to join up at all. It goes without saying that he was the only member of his class at Eton who had chosen to be an imperial policeman. At about this time, records show that on leaving Eton, 57 percent of the students went to Oxford or Cambridge, 20 percent directly into the army, and 16 percent found their next home "in business." Most of those who went straight into business simply joined their fathers' firms.

So, in a way, had Blair. His forebears had gone out to serve the empire. There has been much speculation as to why Eric Blair didn't go on to Oxford or Cambridge. It is usually said that the problem couldn't have been financial—it would have been no trick for him to win a scholarship. But money probably was a factor. He hadn't been an academic star at Eton. He might have been accepted into either of the two great universities simply on the strength of his prior school, but paying the tuition was something else. A full scholarship may not have seemed likely. And even with it there were other costs to be borne. He knew that his father, no longer young and on a permanently fixed income, had made sacrifices to help keep him in Eton, despite his scholarship there. It may well be that Eric Blair did not want to burden his family further.

And he may have been as uncertain as Waugh about which path in life to follow. The choice he made was temporary, but it was defensible. Joining the Indian Imperial Police was several steps up from teaching at a school in Wales that no one had ever heard of. It was also serving one's country. It was very much like what his father had done.

It was a career for which the word "policeman" is misleading. He was an officer in the Imperial Police, and there were only ninety of them in all of Burma, a country of thirteen million. There were, of course, thousands of Burmese and Indians who assisted them, and so much of the work of the British officers was administrative. They did indeed oversee real police work—the capture of murderers, robbers, and so on. But their real function was basically the same as those in the civil service—they were the visible overseers of empire. The entrance exam had nothing whatsoever to do with Burma; it was directed at identifying the proper sort of Englishman, with such essay questions as "Write a letter to a relative about a visit to the theater." Blair also had to write something about Burns, Wordsworth, Scott, or Dickens, and answer the history question, "Who was the greatest prime minister since Pitt?" He had to translate French into English and English into French. His highest grades were in Latin and Greek. He also had to provide an example of freehand drawing and pass a riding test—this last the only practical requirement for police work in Burma.

In Burma, Blair was expected to be the living embodiment of England. It was absolutely essential that he look and behave accordingly. He was required to dress formally for dinner. His uniforms, made by the snubbed tailor in Southwold, cost £150, about the same as Waugh's annual income from teaching and more than Blair's father could easily afford.

When the correctly outfitted young officer arrived in Mandalay for training, he lived within the mile-square walls of Fort Dufferin, which also contained the Upper Burma Club, a polo field, a nine-hole golf course, tennis courts, a chapel, and— other than servants—no Burmese. The much larger community next door, which the maps accurately called the city of Mandalay, was referred to within the Fort as "the native quarter."

Blair spent a year at the Fort, training for the practical aspects of police work, though this instruction did not include actually visiting a police station. There were, however, courses in Burmese, and in these Blair shone. He became fluent in the language. This was considered something of an oddity by his peers, who memorized some words and phrases but habitually addressed the Burmese in English.

Blair was different in other ways as well. He was not a "good mixer," an omission that was considered a major failing. He was considered standoffish, though in fact he was merely a shy and introspective man who wanted time alone. Some thought he was a snob, largely because he had been to Eton. They didn't realize he would have avoided company of any rank. The truth is that as an innately solitary person, he found the social life of the English in the backwoods of the Raj terribly stifling. The same people, the same drinks, the same jokes, the same games at the same club every night. He would rather sit in bed under his mosquito netting and read the latest books from England.

There was one way, though, in which he did fit in. He remained aloof from the Burmese people. Though he spoke their language and even attended some of their religious services, Blair was really no different from any other colonial administrator in his sense of superiority over those whose land he helped to rule. He would come to despise the empire, but more through hatred of its power than affection for its victims.

He spent five years in Burma, and served in many parts of the country. When his training was over he was sent to serve in the alluvial delta town of Myaungmya, compared to which Mandalay was Paris. There were no roads or trains in the remote place in which he now represented the king. He had to travel by boat from one village to another. He traveled with servants—houseman, orderly, cook—and he continued to dress for dinner even when he dined alone in the most remote Dak hut.

He had a number of postings throughout Burma. He received a promotion and now was paid as much as his father had been. He was kept busy—when a murder was committed he would journey to the site and begin the investigation. He saw to it that refineries were guarded. He hunted down bandit gangs.

But it was a desperately lonely life. Some of his colleagues committed suicide and others went mad. It was lonely not merely because he might be the only European within a hundred miles, but because he was in a far-off land whose people did not want him there. The faces he saw were often sullen or mocking. In 1918, Britain had promised constitutional reforms. But by the early 1920s, when Blair arrived, it was clear that these applied to India alone, with Burma being governed in effect by martial law. The British controlled the country's wealth—oil and teak and rice. The Burmese deeply resented these foreign usurpers and being powerless in their own land.

Once, when Blair was rushing to catch a train to take him to the most exclusive British club in Burma, the Gymkhana, some Burmese schoolboys were roughhousing and one of them accidentally bumped into the tall British officer, knocking him down the stairs of the station. Outraged, Blair lifted his heavy cane and was about to strike the boy on the head. At the last minute he gained control of himself and hit the boy on the back instead. The furious boys, and some university undergraduates, too, surrounded Blair and shouted at him. Blair strode on. The young crowd followed him onto the train and rode with him, protesting, until he got off.

Years later, Orwell understood what he and they had become. Everyone in the empire was acting a clearly defined part. He was the aloof and unrepentant oppressor; they were the angry, helpless victims. This perception lies behind Orwell's short story "Shooting an Elephant," which tells us as much about the British Raj as all of Kipling, though coming down on the other side. Orwell based it not on the incident with the mob of schoolboys, but another time and place, when he was called upon to kill a rogue elephant. When the imperial policeman in his story arrives, he sees at once that the beast has calmed down and is no longer dangerous. But he kills it anyway. He does so because he sees all those native faces *expecting* him to do so. That was his role. Passive, even hostile, observation was theirs. Everyone did what was expected, and that was the essence of an empire and what allowed it to work.

One of Blair's postings was in Rangoon, the new capital in the southern and more tropical part of the country. It was a real city; there were good restaurants and occasional visitors from home, including an old Etonian, Christopher Hollis, who was touring the world as a debater for the Oxford Union. There was other company available in Rangoon—Blair frequented the waterfront brothels and found diversion in a local book-shop, Smart and Mookudin's, reading magazines and books from home.

Other postings followed. He saw his grandmother. He jour-neyed from one station to the next. He did his work. And he never stopped acting his cold imperial part—or even believing it. He did what his country wanted him to, including resenting the Burmese for not being British. Later he wrote that at the time he thought "the greatest joy in the world would be to drive a bayonet into a Buddhist priest's guts."

And then, in 1927, after five years in Burma, Blair returned to England and resigned from the service.

Many still wonder why he went to Burma at all. And there is equal puzzlement as to why he left. It is sometimes assumed, given his later politics and writing, that he had become dis-gusted by the empire and so fled from its service.

It is not that simple. He probably went to Burma because his schoolmates had taught him to remain in his "place," and so he chose the kind of work that his father had done. When he left Burma he had no philosophy and no plan other than to become a writer. "Become" is apt, because he had written virtually nothing and had shown no great promise at the craft he was now determined to make his life's work.

What had happened to him was Burma. He had spent five lonely years with his books and his thoughts. Many who leave their mark in life have reached their path through isolation. Blair had been cut off from everything he knew, and so he came to know himself. He had begun to think. From his imperial cocoon came transformation. The policeman became a writer.

Back in England, the ruminations of five closed-off years produced in Blair his destiny. He now could see his homeland with fresh eyes. He saw with great clarity his nation's social ladder but resolved never to climb it. He chose to close the door completely on the possibility of conventional success. "I felt that I had to escape not merely from imperialism, but from every form of man's dominion over man," he later wrote. "Failure seemed to me the only true virtue. Every suspicion of self-advancement, even to 'succeed' in life to the extent of making a few hundreds a year, seemed to me spiritually ugly, a species of bullying."

And so, at the time Waugh was struggling to climb upward, Eric Blair began to move down the sharp hill that led to all the years ahead.

Mr. Toad on Top

—

THE STORY OF EVELYN WAUGH'S QUEST FOR A BRIDE is very much a part of his quest for status, too. It is a tale of obstinacy, perseverance, resourcefulness, and eventual success that outdoes Stanley's search for Livingston. Waugh sought a marriage that would bring him to the top of the hill that he had begun to climb when the jellyfish had changed his plans from suicide to self-promotion.

The hill seemed steepest at the bottom. When he first left Oxford, before teaching in Wales, he realized that while he had befriended many of the rich or titled, he did not know their families. He received invitations to the London apartments of his former classmates, but not to their parents' estates.

But one wellborn family did make him welcome on its own turf, and the experience changed his life. In his last year at Oxford, Waugh met the Plunket Greene brothers. It would have been hard to miss them. Waugh appreciated languor, frivolity, and height, and the Plunket Greenes were almost a parody of these traits. David (whose heroin addiction eventually led to his suicide) was just under seven feet tall. This did not prevent Waugh from getting into a fight with him the very first time they met, at a party at Oxford. Not surprisingly, he grew closer to the younger Plunket Greene brother, Richard, who was good-looking, a heavy drinker, and mad about jazz.

David and Richard Plunket Greene lived with their mother, Gwen (who was separated from their father), and their sister, Olivia. They invited Waugh to visit. This was his great chance not merely to observe the scions of the upper class but actually to fraternize with their families. He did not waste the opportunity.

Gwen Plunket Greene was the daughter of Sir Charles Hubert Hastings Parry, composer of the great hymn "Jerusalem," and Lady Maude Herbert, sister of the thirteenth Earl of Pembroke. Her elder sister married the prominent aristocrat Arthur Ponsonby, who later became Lord Ponsonby of Shulbrede. These connections were, of course, well-known to Waugh when he came to call.

To put it mildly, he was enraptured. "I fell in love with an entire family," Waugh later wrote, and directed "the sentiment upon the only appropriate member, an eighteen-year-old daughter." Actually, she was only seventeen.

Waugh's diary was slightly inaccurate. He *did* fall in love with an entire family. It became the great passion of his life. But it was not the Plunket Greenes with whom he fell in love. It was the Herbert family.

From Olivia, Waugh learned the full luster of that surname. Deriding the Plunket Greenes as "bog Irish," she informed her eager suitor and pupil that the highest place in social heaven belonged to her mother's family, the Herberts. "Her maternal grandmother had been a Herbert," wrote Selena Hastings, a Waugh biographer and herself an aristocrat, "and she had inherited to the full the Herbert pride in the Herbert name, the belief that Herbert blood was of an inherently superior quality to that which ran in the veins of other great English families . . . her character traits, she was convinced, deriving from the Woronzow connection that had been made at the beginning of the nineteenth century when a daughter of Count Woronzow had married the Earl of Pembroke, head of the Herbert family."

Waugh was ecstatic. He had found the holy grail. The Herberts were the very top of the upper class. Olivia was a Herbert. He desperately wanted to marry her.

There were a few problems. The absence of either money or career were not even at the top of the list of his disabilities. First, as always, was the matter of social class. When Olivia or her mother wished to express their strongest disdain, the terms they used were "middle-class" and "second-rate." Olivia left no doubt that Waugh was the perfect example of both. And the sexual gulf between them was even greater than the social. Olivia, unfettered by middle-class restraint, was wildly promiscuous. Despite her snobbery in everything else, she was an equal opportunity seducer of men, regardless of race, creed, or social status. (She did prefer men of talent, as with Paul Robeson.) But her conquests, however varied, did not include Waugh. She found him unappealing in that regard, and thought him ridiculously inexperienced, which, at the time, with women at least, he was. She also considered herself to be far beyond him intellectually, and much better read.

None of this discouraged his pursuit. There was not enough cold water to dampen the fact that she was a Herbert. His ardor was like a force of nature. He was always in her company.

We must ask why she permitted his constant presence. For one thing, she saw early on that he could become a great writer. And she loved to be amused. Waugh, when he wanted to, could be the most amusing man on earth, and with Olivia he wanted to. Moreover, she drank as heavily as he did, so they had something to do together. With wit and pranks he made her roar with laughter.

She recognized how gifted he was. When she heard, in January 1925, that he was going to Wales to be a schoolmaster, she rushed to Underhill in Golders Green to tell him that he was a great artist, and that he mustn't become a teacher.

But he did. He had to. He had been living on his parents' money and it just ran out. He had agreed to teach school, and when it came time to do so, he went.

Whenever he could get away, he rushed to London to pursue Olivia, but he was no more successful than before. However much she had come to respect his talent, there was still the barrier of social class. They were both reminded that he didn't belong in her world. While Waugh was being driven to a party at the Plunket Greenes by Olivia's cousin Matthew Ponsonby, both of them drunk, police stopped the car for driving the wrong way around a traffic circle in the middle of the Strand. The young men were thrown into jail cells. Matthew's father, Arthur Ponsonby, who until recently had been secretary of state for foreign affairs, quietly saw to it that his son was released on bail but did nothing for Waugh, who sat in his cell for four hours and then paid a fine.

The incident did not endear Waugh to the Plunket Greenes, who seemed to blame him rather than their relative who had been at the wheel. That, and the failure to offer bail, left Waugh no doubt as to where he stood. He was a nobody. Even the newspaper account of the episode, while mentioning Ponsonby, referred to Waugh merely as "another man in the car who was incapably drunk." Olivia continued to save her favors for others. Waugh slunk back to teaching.

But not at the same place. He had resigned from Arnold when he thought he would land a job in Italy. When that fell through, he found a teaching job at another school, Aston Clinton in Buckinghamshire, much closer to his two loves, Oxford and Olivia.

With distance no barrier, his courtship of the family intensified. When Richard Plunket Greene married Elizabeth Russell, whose great-grandfather was the Duke of Bedford, Waugh served as his best man. And now that he was relatively close to London, he was able to woo and win over their astonishing circle of friends as well.

The young Plunket Greenes knew all the Bright Young People, the name journalists affixed to the most fashionable set of partygoers whenever they made it into the headlines, which was virtually every day.

So every time he could escape from school for revels with town or gown, he did so. Richard Plunket Greene gave him a motorcycle and on this he dashed to London or Oxford, returning to Aston Clinton against all odds in a state of extreme drunkenness. This did not escape notice, and he was eventually asked to leave the school.

He found yet another teaching job, but this one really was the bottom of the barrel. For £5 a week he taught at a school in Notting Hill that aspired to become third-rate. He continued to court Olivia, who had developed a fierce if surprising enthusiasm for the Catholic Church. She particularly liked the idea of mortification of the flesh. Apparently the only time she ever respected Waugh was when he jabbed a lighted cigarette into her wrist.

Waugh was not living an enviable life. But at this lowest of low points everything suddenly changed. The future for the first time began to brighten.

Somehow, in his few hours of sobriety, he started to write and published two stories. Even better, Duckworth, a major publisher, commissioned him to write a biography of the painter Dante Gabriel Rossetti for the upcoming centenary of the artist's birth. It was a small start, but it was a start. His favorite expression when things were going well was "Mr. Toad on Top," an allusion to Kenneth Grahame's *The Wind in the Willows*, one of his favorite books, and now he was able to use the phrase more often. He found a new and much better job, writing for the London *Daily Express*. Things were starting to happen.

Sometimes he went to parties to which he hadn't actually been invited, and at one of the best of these, in April 1927, he met a striking young woman. All of a sudden, Olivia was a thing of the past. Waugh now was transfixed by Evelyn Gardner. There was something wonderful about her name. No, not her first name, even though it was the same as his. Nor her last name. Nothing special about Gardner. Rather, it was her mother's maiden name—Herbert. For Evelyn Gardner was also a member of the Herbert family, Waugh's north star.

In fact, she was more a Herbert than Olivia had been. How could it be more perfect? Waugh, to whom Debrett's was the true bible, knew at once just who Evelyn Gardner was.

Her uncle, the fifth Earl of Carnarvon, had discovered King Tut's tomb and thus supposedly unleashed its curse. He had entered the antechamber of the tomb in February 1923 and by early April he was dead of a mosquito bite, which gave the ancient warning some credence in the modern world.

Evelyn Gardner's mother was the eldest daughter of the fourth Earl of Carnarvon, and so was a sister of the victim of the curse. Miss Gardner's father, the first Baron Burghclere, was deceased, and now the household was headed by the Dowager Lady Burghclere.

Actually, it seemed less a household than a monarchy. Lady Burghclere's rule was absolute. She needed no title to suggest the imperious and forceful stage caricature of a dowager. She was not to be trifled with. She had four children, all daughters, which meant that her title would lapse, and she is said to have named the fourth girl Evelyn because it at least *suggested* a man's name. Not that daughters weren't useful—they could be married off to very rich men, which in two cases had already been accomplished. She had the same goal for Evelyn.

But her daughter seemed to have no goals at all, save escape from her mother's control. The way to do this was through marriage—but one of her own choosing. People called her "pretty" (never "beautiful"—she was too boyish in appearance for that), and her slim androgynous figure and short hair were exactly right for the flapper era. She had no trouble attracting men but was quite indecisive thereafter. She had already been engaged nine times, it was said, when she met Waugh. (When Lady Burghclere tried to break up one engagement by sending her daughter on a voyage to Australia, Evelyn returned engaged to the ship's purser.)

As soon as Waugh met her, his campaign was on. He took her to restaurants that were completely beyond his means. They were seen together everywhere. Their friends referred to them as "He-Evelyn" and "She-Evelyn" in order to gossip about them without confusion.

True, he was penniless, but she found it hard to resist his magnetism and wit. She liked to be amused, and Waugh was, for her, very, very amusing. She saw that he was a unique, highly gifted artist, and she respected that. She was probably quite bright herself, though that was hard to tell because she spoke in the baby talk so popular in her set. (She referred to Marcel Proust as "Prousty-wousty" and was so favorably impressed by He-Evelyn's father that she declared, "Old Mr. Waugh is a complete Pinkle-Wonk.") It is difficult to imagine what the two Evelyns' conversations were like. Her life was frivolous, given over almost entirely to parties, and she was enthusiastic all the time. He most definitely was not. It was a strange romance.

One night he proposed. He had taken her to dinner at the Ritz. Though he would be lauded as the greatest wordsmith of his time, all he could come up with in asking her to marry him was "Why don't we try it and see how it goes?" She-Evelyn, who had received so many proposals before, recognized a new low. She told him she wanted to think it over.

The next morning she phoned him and said yes. Her roommate was likely to be married soon, which would mean She-Evelyn's return to her mother's domain. Only marriage could prevent that. And "yes," after all, was her habitual response.

When news of the engagement reached the Dowager Lady Burghclere, she went into her full battle mode. None of those other fiancés had met all the dowager's standards, but Waugh struck her as unacceptable on every count.

She gathered her ammunition. She made the journey to Oxford in order to search for more information about young Mr. Waugh. She found it. Her informant was our old friend Dean Cruttwell, still smarting from the canine slander. He was only too happy to tell Lady Burghclere all that he knew, which was plenty.

Thus armed with tales of continual drunkenness, "*ces vices*," filial ingratitude, poverty, debt, general degeneracy, and a father "virtually in trade," she summoned Waugh to her home, where she informed him that he was an impossible choice for her daughter.

Lady Burghclere was more than a match for any man in England except Evelyn Waugh in his quest for a Herbert bride. He stared her down. If this was the way she was going to be, he said, then the Evelyns would be married within the week.

She realized he meant it. So she regrouped and agreed to a wedding in September, but on one condition: Waugh first had to find a job. And not just sporadic journalism. He had to be employed full-time.

This he set out to do. He talked to friends and applied for positions. He really wanted a steady income, because he really wanted to marry Evelyn Gardner. But all the same he knew by now what he was put on earth to be. He was going to be a writer, and, unlike so many with a similar self-image, he set out to prove it by actually writing.

Despite parties and courtship, sporadic jobs and steady drinking, he finished his book on Rossetti, dedicating it to Evelyn Gardner. ("She-Evelyn" would have been a little over the top). *Rossetti* was generally well-received, though of course it was not meant to be, and never became, a bestseller. Its reception was good enough for Waugh's publisher, Duckworth, to urge him to write a novel.

He was already well along with one. Authors are supposed to write about what they know, and so Waugh wrote the story of a young man who teaches at a ghastly boarding school in Wales who then comes to London and enters high society. His notes for the novel were his diary. He had wisely decided to write a funny book. In its pages his teaching days were exorcised; they were made comic. Even the perverted instructor who preyed upon students at Arnold House was in the book, bigger and buggier than life and somehow hilarious.

Even before the book was published, those who saw the finished chapters roared with laughter. They couldn't wait for more, and Waugh wrote at a feverish pace.

He was able to devote so much time to writing because he still had no permanent job. He had tried to keep his bargain with Lady Burghclere, but something always kept him from employment. Little did he know that that something was Lady Burghclere. She had powerful friends. When Waugh was about to be hired by the BBC, she saw to it that the offer was withdrawn.

And when he finished his novel and took it to Duckworth, there was trouble there, too. Lady Burghclere's sister was married to Sir George Duckworth, whose brother Gerald was Waugh's publisher. He insisted on so many changes in the (admittedly scandalous) text that Waugh, as intended, withdrew his manuscript and left.

Lady Burghclere probably hoped that by this point the author would jump off London Bridge, but she must have forgotten about the father "in trade." Though it was probably painful to do so, Waugh took his text to his father's publishing house. Chapman & Hall was pleased to accept it, but also insisted on many changes. This time Waugh agreed. He really wanted to marry that girl.

And marry her he did, without her mother's knowledge. At noon on June 27, 1928, in an unfashionable church in Portman Square, with a woman typing away on the altar, a cockney curate performed the ceremony from which emerged two Evelyn Waughs, man and wife.

Lady Burghclere was not told until three weeks later. She

was very angry. She was icy and defiant. But she was no fool. There was now nothing she could do but put a notice in *The Times,* which she quickly did. Since they were living together, people should at least be told that they were married.

The young couple set up housekeeping in a small flat that cost them only £1 a week. Waugh's novel was coming out soon and all their hopes were on that, though Waugh was having trouble thinking of a title.

He finally decided on *Decline and Fall,* and they needn't have worried. Soon after its publication it was in its third printing. The reviews were good, too. Oxford connections helped, of course, as when Cyril Connolly wrote in the *New Statesman,* "though not a great book, it is a funny book; the only one that professionally I have ever read twice." But the novelist Arnold Bennett hadn't been to Oxford with Waugh, or indeed at all, and as a Grand Old Man of English Literature his review was very important; he wrote, "*Decline and Fall* is an uncompromising and brilliantly malicious satire, which in my opinion comes near to being quite first rate."

"Comes *near*"? "Not a great book"? Everybody loved it, and everybody laughed, and the book sold very well. But the critics weren't certain that a comic novel could also be a work of genius. Waugh would eventually remove all doubt on that score.

In the meantime, he had been launched. And most successfully. The literary world, then and now, was small and inbred, and its opinion leaders few in number. And now this elite group that controlled which books were bought were all for Waugh. Not a genius, it was at first thought, but a scream. He was asked to meet literary lions Max Beerbohm, Hilaire Belloc, and Maurice Baring—all in one evening. There were more parties than ever, and now he was not the son of a publisher from Golders Green, nor even just the bridegroom of an aristocrat. He was an up-and-coming author and the wittiest man in town.

And he was solvent. Magazines and newspapers paid well for brief articles, preferably on the younger generation, since the hero of *Decline and Fall* was about the same age as its author. His publisher wanted another novel, hopefully about the fashionable younger set as well.

Waugh was becoming entrenched within the crowd whose astonishing members would people his pages as long as he lived. Marrying a Herbert had indeed paid off socially. She-Evelyn's debutante friends turned out to be a priceless dowry. Waugh had gained access to the very inner circle, and was to become its center. His dazzling coterie of friends would become as much a part of his legend as his books.

There is no better example than the Mitfords. They were a set of their own, and not even Waugh could invent characters to match them. The first Mitford he met was probably Nancy, who was a close friend of his wife. Nancy was one of the six daughters of Baron Redesdale, all of whom became friends of Waugh, as did their only brother, Tom. She became a celebrated author and maintained a long and delightful correspondence with Waugh.

Nancy's sister Diana Mitford had married Bryan Guinness, heir to the beer fortune and immensely rich. (Waugh already knew him; they had been fellow members of the Oxford Railway Club.) Diana was astonishingly, famously beautiful, and the young Guinnesses were the couple everyone wanted to meet. Waugh became, for a while, practically a member of this household. (Diana would eventually divorce Guinness to marry Sir Oswald Mosley, the head of the British Union of Fascists—in effect the English Nazi party. They were married in Berlin, in Joseph Goebbels's apartment, with only a few friends, including the führer, in attendance. The Mosleys were imprisoned in England during World War II.) Another sister, Unity Valkyrie Mitford, fell madly in love with Adolf Hitler and moved to Germany to be in his company, which she often was. "The greatest moment of my life was sitting at Hitler's feet and having him stroke my hair," she once said. When Germany and England went to war in 1939, she shot herself. But the Mitfords were not confined to only one end of the political spectrum. Another sister, Jessica ("Decca"), moved to America and joined the Communist Party.* (She later wrote a bestseller.) Still another sister, Deborah, became the Duchess of Devonshire.

However unusual the Mitfords may have seemed, they were in a sense among Waugh's more conventional friends, in that they actually *had* political views, however extreme, foolish, or, in some cases, evil; they wrote books, which is to say they did *something;* and they conducted themselves much like aristocrats had in the past, not like their young peers were behaving at present. They were unique among Waugh's new circle because they did not devote all of their time to going to parties.

Much closer to the festive norm was, for example, Baby Jungman, whose real name was Theresa. Even more than She-Evelyn, she was the prototype of the Bright Young People. The

---

* She had some trouble joining. The party member application form asked "Occupation of father." She wanted to answer truthfully by writing "Peer of the Realm" but suspected that her comrades wouldn't like that. Then she remembered that Lord Redesdale owned a gold mine in, of all places, Swastika, Ontario, and so she relievedly wrote down "miner" on the form. (Her father, whenever required to state his occupation, always answered with the single word "Honourable.")

daughter of Mrs. Richard Guinness, she lived a life seemingly dedicated to parties and pranks. At age fifteen she passed herself off in London society as Madame Anna Vorolsky, a Russian refugee forced to sell her jewels to pay "for the education of my poor little boy." Her remarkable costume, enhanced by fake pearls and her mother's mink coat, plus a bravura accent, allowed her to pull off the *russe* ruse with astonishing success. The Duke of Marlborough was completely taken in and expressed his deepest compassion for "your ravaged country."

Spurred by this success, Baby pushed the envelope. She appeared at a fashionable garden party leading two borzois on a chain. Presented as Mme. Vorolsky to a distinguished and elderly general, she spoke to him with heavily accented passion.

"Oh Seer Enry—Navair shall I forget that *wonderful* night we spent together in Paris in the war."

The General flushed and looked anxiously at his wife.

"To the best of my recollection, madame," he replied coldly, "I spent only one night in Paris in the whole war."

"Zat," replied Baby archly, "was zee night."

The general retreated.

Another leader of the Bright Young People was Elizabeth Ponsonby, a cousin of Olivia Plunket Greene. Each had been described as an Oxford "camp-follower." Even then, it was recalled, "Elizabeth Ponsonby, a typical product of the age, recklessly charged at life, creating chaos around her." She seemed to do this full-time in London throughout the twenties. She couldn't very well entertain in the "new" way at home, since she lived with her parents in St. James's Palace (her father held a position close to the king), and so she sought alternative venues. In July 1928, she was censured by the London press for a party she had cohosted at St. George's Swimming Baths, whose pool was commandeered for the occasion. The dress code for the dance, which began at the usual hour of eleven at night, was bathing suits, though some eventually wore less than that. The night was warm, the music hot, the Bathwater Cocktail (invented for the occasion and served by bartenders as scantily dressed as the guests) was potent, and the dawn completely ignored. The departing guests, who by then were quite a sight, drew hostile stares from laborers on their way to work.

Waugh was not at all these parties, but he knew of them from friends and from the company and columns of Tom Driberg, a classmate at both Lancing and Oxford, and now a busy gossip columnist for the *Daily Express*. There was almost too much to tell. On the eve of Lord Faringdon's wedding, the guests poured gallons of gasoline into the river and set the Thames on fire.

All these privileged people with nothing else to do frantically sought new themes for their revels. They required a new set for each performance, though the cast was always the same. There was a highly publicized Mozart party, in which everyone wore eighteenth-century costume. There was a circus party. Fifteen bachelors in Lancaster Gate gave a Wild West party. ("Our English servants gave notice.") There was a sailor party and a baby party. Diana Guinness gave an 1860s party. There were impersonation parties: "Come as somebody else," "Come as your dearest enemy," "Come as your secret self." There was a party where everyone had to dress as some other guest at the party. (Oliver Messel went as Tallulah Bankhead.)

Treasure hunts were very big, too. The Bright Young People followed the clues all over town. When one clue was hidden near Buckingham Palace, the captain of the King's Guard, believing the palace was under siege, turned out all his troops and sent for reinforcements.

There were elaborate hoaxes, as well. The most celebrated of these involved an exhibition of paintings by one Bruno Hat, a German painter of abstract art, "seemingly derivative of Picasso and Chirico." The exhibition was packed with art critics, journalists, and, of course, the BYP. The eminent Bloomsburian Lytton Strachey bought one of the canvases.

There was, in fact, no Bruno Hat. Brian Howard painted the artwork. Waugh wrote the preface to the catalog. Bryan Guinness helped stage the event, and Tom Mitford, wearing dark glasses and a false mustache and sitting in a wheelchair, very successfully carried off his impersonation of Bruno Hat. (Being a Mitford, he spoke flawless German.)

In his book on society in this period, Nicholas Courtney defines the Bright Young People as "the generic term for any decadent members of the younger generation who behaved badly, or irresponsibly, during the latter half of the 1920s." If they live on even now it is because they were the principal characters in Evelyn Waugh's second novel, which caused a sensation.

Vile Bodies is a book about the Bright Young People—and a great deal more. It is an astonishing portrayal of the hedonism and nihilism of a generation that sensed far better than its elders that their carefree days were merely an interregnum between two savage global slaughters. It is about the vacuity of life without faith.

But the glittering surface of the book garnered the most attention. The vast public that bought illustrated dailies to revel vicariously with the golden youth could now enjoy their company between the covers in more scintillating detail. In the world to which his Herbert wife gave him access, Waugh had been not merely ubiquitous but attentive. He had soaked up everything. At the Guinnesses' he heard the way these people talked, and he parroted it perfectly in his pages. It is hard to believe that grown-up, educated people spoke this way. Embarrassment was called "shy-making"; spoiled food, or sometimes cocaine, was "ill-making"; the right medication was "very better making"; opening wide the drapes while still hungover was "blind-making." There were endless possibilities. And the rest of these conversations were no better. Most spoken words were expressions of disdain, such as "this really is all too bogus," or "how too, too shaming."

Then there were the parties, exhaustively recorded in the press but which in *Vile Bodies* are filtered through Waugh's rhythmic concision, so that gossip becomes art.

Mixed parties, Savage parties, Victorian parties, Greek parties, Wild West parties, Russian parties, Circus parties, parties where one had to dress as somebody else, almost naked parties in St. John's Wood, parties in flats and studios and houses and ships and hotels and night clubs, in windmills and swimming baths, tea parties at school where one ate muffins and meringues and tinned crab, parties at Oxford where one drank brown sherry and smoked Turkish cigarettes, dull dances in London and comic dances in Scotland and disgusting dances in Paris—all that succession and repetition of massed humanity. . . . Those vile bodies.

There is much more to the book than a chronicle of degeneracy. It is an indictment of a whole society.

And there is a great and growing mastery of the English language. The use of dialogue is amazing, but there is much more to the work than that. Waugh seems blessed by the gods to write sublimely. It was as if he needed merely to place his pen on paper to see the ink expand and spread across the page in glorious design. There is no more sure and subtle craftsman of the English language. There is a scene in *Vile Bodies* in which a gossip columnist, young Lord Balcairn, commits suicide because he's been barred from a party. Waugh bids him farewell: "So the last Earl of Balcairn went, as they say, to his fathers (who had fallen in many lands and for many causes, as the eccentricities of British Foreign Policy and their own wandering natures had directed them, at Acre and Agincourt and Killiecrankie, in Egypt and America. One had been pulled white by fishes as the tides rolled him among the tree-tops of a submarine forest; some had grown black and unfit for consideration under tropical suns; while many of them lay in marble tombs of extravagant design)."

But what drew most people's attention was the sex and scandal in the book. Readers tried to figure out who the real-life models for Waugh's characters might be. "People bought the book as an adjunct to their romantic absorption in gossip columns."

At its heart, this "funny" book contains a bleak worldview. It makes it clear that the pointless frenzy of its fashionable young characters is the result of a moral void. There was no religion in their lives, no faith and no hereafter, and so there was nothing to live for but fleeting pleasure.

(*Vile Bodies* accepts as a given that life is unfair. Virtue goes unrewarded and the strong triumph. The last pages of the novel, with the world becoming a devastated battlefield, are quite as hopeless as the conclusion of *1984*. The aimlessness of life without faith, the impossibility of living without tradition, the absence of fairness, the triumph of might—all these "Orwellian" themes are struck as well by Waugh in even one of his most frivolous comic novels.)

Vile Bodies sold very well indeed. *Decline and Fall* had shown Waugh to be a writer of promise. *Vile Bodies* made him a star. It came out in January 1930, and by October was in its eleventh edition. Everyone talked about it. Major newspapers begged Waugh for articles, offering stupendous fees. *Decline and Fall* was rushed back to the bookstores to cash in on Waugh's new fame. He recorded in his diary an income of £2,500, and for the first time Waugh felt rich.

More important than money were all the new invitations. There were more parties than ever, and once-formidable doors were now open. The most fashionable hostesses fought over him: Lady Colefax, Lady Cunard, and Mrs. Laura Corrigan, an American with no title but who could and sometimes did spend £6,000 on a single party. At the age of twenty-six, Evelyn Waugh's most ambitious dreams had come true.

He should have been euphoric. He was, in fact, heartbroken. "I didn't know that it was possible to be so miserable and live."

The cause of his terrible pain was She-Evelyn's infidelity. It was the same old story of Couples Who Never Should Have Gotten Married in the First Place. She-Evelyn had met another man, John Heygate. He had been to Eton with Orwell and Oxford with Waugh and was now working as news editor at the BBC. He was tall and good-looking and fun to be with.

And Waugh was not around. He had been working furiously to finish *Vile Bodies*. All too aware of how susceptible he was to social distractions, throughout his life he would hole up in some isolated spot (often a hotel) when he was writing. In this case he went to Oxfordshire.

She-Evelyn was left alone. Nancy Mitford moved into the Waughs' spare room to keep her company, but this was not sufficient for the restless Mrs. Waugh. Her husband loved parties as much as she, but they had proved to be secondary to his work. To She-Evelyn, parties were secondary to nothing. She went out every night. John Heygate was available as an escort. Waugh was somewhere in Oxfordshire. What was likely to happen, happened.

In July 1929, though engrossed in his work, Waugh made a quick trip back to London, where his wife informed him that she and Heygate were having an affair and were in love.

Waugh was completely devastated. He was stunned and hurt and angry. His soul was seared with bitterness that would last throughout his life. And it was the pain and humiliation of a public rejection that mattered more to him than the loss of a tentative wife.

He was halfway through *Vile Bodies* when he heard the news, and it is easy to see the change in the book's tone. The last chapter is about as bleak and nihilistic as anything ever written. Waugh even gave it a sarcastic title—"Happy Ending," though the other chapters are merely numbered. (When a film was made of the book in 2003, titled *Bright Young Things*, an actual happy ending was substituted in order to avoid depressing the audience.)

The Waughs made a few stabs at reconciliation, but that was all they were—stabs. On January 18, 1930, they were divorced. It was customary in such situations for the wife to be allowed to divorce the husband, regardless of who had been the adulterer. But She-Evelyn insisted that he divorce her, since her actions had caused the breach. He was in complete agreement. After the divorce, she married Heygate, becoming the first of his three wives.

One might think that it was impossible even for Waugh to express the full force of the pain caused by his wife's infidelity, except that he found a way to do so. Five years and several books later, in *A Handful of Dust*, he describes an adulterous wife and places her in what might well be the most chilling scene in English literature. The wife's lover (like She-Evelyn's) is named John. Her son is named John Andrew. The lover is on a plane trip, and she is worried about him. The young son is killed in a hunting accident near their country estate, Hetton. The grieving husband sends a family friend to break the news to his wife in person. She is called out from a party and sees the friend's anguished look.

"What is it, Jack? Tell me quickly, I'm scared. It's nothing awful is it?"

"I'm afraid it is. There's been a very serious accident."

"John?"

"Yes."

"Dead?"

He nodded.

She sat down on a hard little Empire chair against the wall, perfectly still with her hands folded in her lap, like a small well-brought-up child introduced into a room full of grown-ups. She said, "Tell me what happened? Why do you know about it first?"

"I've been down to Hetton since the week-end."

"Hetton?"

"Don't you remember? John was going hunting today."

She frowned, not at once taking in what he was saying. "John . . . John Andrew . . . I . . . Oh thank God . . ." Then she burst into tears.

He got her. Whether or not any mother, even in the throes of an affair, actually would have said, "Oh thank God," on learning of her little boy's death, he got her. Waugh's reaction to being hurt was to strike back harder. When faced with a bully, he became a worse bully. The hurt of his divorce made him tougher and more acerbic than he had ever been before.

So Waugh was the toast of London, though badly burned. He was rich and famous, but he walked through parties like a caustic zombie. He was afraid that people were laughing at him. He was in pain. His wit grew more cruel, which many previously had not thought possible. He had lost his wife and he had lost his Herbert connection.

He managed to find a perfectly good substitute for both. As soon as his wife told him the bad news, he fled to the hearth of Bryan and Diana Guinness for comfort. Actually, several hearths, as the Guinnesses had many homes—in London, in Paris, in the country, and a very grand estate just off Phoenix Park in Dublin. He was welcome to stay at all these places, and stay he did. He was like a member of the family. The Guinnesses were not Herberts, of course, but being the richest man and most beautiful woman in England was, after all, *something*.

Bryan Guinness was busy studying for the bar. Diana Mitford Guinness, nineteen and pregnant, stayed close to her home(s) and wanted company, and so Waugh became her constant companion, chatting or reading to her as she rested, eating his dinner at a little table at the end of her bed.

Waugh fell in love with her. All his passion was directed toward an aristocratic ideal, and now she was it. His feelings were not reciprocated. She was probably unaware of them. She welcomed Waugh's company because he was amusing, and she liked to be amused. In a sense, that's what she lived for. Fun and laughter weren't trifles, they were the affirmation of an aristocratic resolve to wring pleasure out of every moment. (When, during the Second World War, as the wife of Oswald Mosley, Diana was imprisoned for years under very harsh conditions, she still kept to the code. "We've never had such laughs since Lady Mosley left," recalled one of the matrons at her prison.)

Waugh didn't laugh. He made others laugh. After her first child was born, Diana returned to the busy London social scene. She didn't drop Waugh, but now there were others who could amuse her. There was dancing and music and travel. He no longer could be part of her daily life.

Her unavailability was to him like a second divorce. He was deeply embittered. He had dedicated *Vile Bodies* to Bryan and Diana Guinness and given its manuscript to them as a Christmas present. (In 1984, at Christie's, it sold for £55,000.) And now Diana dared to have *other friends*, people with whom she spent most of her time.

It was childish, of course, but it caused a rift in their friendship that never healed.

It was some consolation to remember that there were other fish in the sea. Diana Guinness was married, but there were a number of highly eligible young women in London who were not. Waugh was young, famous, attractive, seemingly rich, a social lion, and now unattached. It would not have been difficult to find a beautiful heiress willing to join him on his upward path through life.

He fell in love with the very rich Baby Jungman, who, despite her leadership of the Bright Young People, was intelligent and sensitive.

But he couldn't ask her to marry him. He couldn't marry anyone, because, to the shock of almost all who knew him, he had been received into the Roman Catholic Church.

The pain of a failed marriage had caused him to take a hard look at his life. His mind came to see what his pen had known from the start—that the life he was living was empty, devoid of plan or point. So he chose order in this life and salvation in the next. He remained thereafter an exceptionally devout acolyte of his faith.

Conversion may have changed his faith but not his manners. He continued wantonly to insult and astound. Nor did his devotion to the Church of Rome have any effect on his social climbing. When Waugh was received into the church, on September 29, 1930, he brought only one witness to the ceremony, Tom Driberg, his classmate from Lancing and Oxford. It was a curious choice, as Driberg was devoutly Anglican. But he was also a gossip columnist for the London *Daily Express.* And sure enough, the next morning Driberg's column, reporting on a new black singer from America, noted that in addition to other glitterati in the audience—Lady Ravensdale, Tallulah Bankhead, the Marquis of Casa Maury—"watching intently from the balcony was Mr. Evelyn Waugh, who had earlier in the evening been received into the Roman Catholic church." Just because one has become a lamb of Christ doesn't mean that one must leave the social fold.

But to Waugh, religion, if it came to that, *was* more important even than social climbing. It was more important literally than anything on earth.

Many commentators have been puzzled by his religious fervor and fealty. It seems to them at odds with his flamboyant lifestyle. Some try to explain this by saying he had an inherently religious nature. When Waugh was a boy (in a Church of England household) his father observed that his younger son seemed to be spending his time "serving at the altar, & going to picnics—a weird mixture of faith and frivolity."

But Waugh strongly denied that he had known real faith before joining the Catholic Church. "The shallowness of my early piety is shown by the ease with which I abandoned it," he noted. Further, and this is the key to his conversion, it was the frivolity that had driven him to faith. "Those of you who have read my books," he wrote in 1949, "will perhaps understand the character of the world into which I exuberantly launched myself. Ten years of that world sufficed to show one that life there, or anywhere, was unintelligible or unendurable without God." It therefore was with "a firm intellectual conviction but with little emotion [that] I was admitted into the Church. My life since then has been an endless delightful tour of discovery in the huge area of which I was made free."

Waugh believed that life without a moral code was chaos, that Christianity provided the moral code on which Western civilization rested, and that Catholicism was the purest form of Christianity. His faith was indeed a rational, not an emotional, choice, and it brought order and purpose to his life.

He adhered strictly to the tenets of his faith, regardless of their effect on his social aspirations. He had knowingly joined a church that did not recognize divorce, and so in the eyes of that church and therefore in his own mind as well, Waugh was still married. As long as Evelyn Gardner lived, he could not marry again. This precluded any future with an heiress. And if he *were* free to marry, it would have to be to someone of his own faith. Most of the aristocracy, from the Herberts on down, were Protestants.

So Waugh, having upon conversion surrendered his right to remarry, now had to choose between celibacy and the confessional. At least, as it happened, he could avoid having to confess to his own priest. He began to travel to exotic far-off lands. He attended the coronation of Haile Selassie in Ethiopia (then called Abyssinia by the British). He visited the country several times. (And got two hilarious books out of it: *Black Mischief* and *Scoop.*) He went to British Guiana and Brazil and Morocco and the Arctic. He recovered in Venice and Portofino.

He also spent considerable time in the noble homes of England. It was only a matter of time before Waugh, who seldom met a country house he didn't like, arrived at Pixton, the Georgian seat of one branch of the Herbert family. It was a very high branch. And these Herberts were different in one regard from the others he had known. The head of the family, Mary Herbert, widow of the second son of the fourth Earl of Carnarvon, had converted to the Roman Catholic Church. And so had her daughters. One of these daughters was named Laura. Waugh fell in love with her. She was very young but self-possessed. She was quiet, thoughtful, completely unpretentious, attractive, kind, and gentle. And, of course, she was a Herbert. She was, as if a gift from God for Waugh's conversion, a Catholic Herbert.

But if she was eligible for marriage, he was not. In the eyes of their church he was still married to her cousin She-Evelyn.

He was, however, working on that. Waugh had begun the process of obtaining an annulment. He must have loved the word. Annulment. *Annul.* To make the marriage void, as if it had never happened. He could be both single and undivorced. Then he could marry again. He could marry another Herbert.

If, that is, he could obtain an annulment. His Anglican friends told him that it was a cinch. Many English Protestants believed the Church of Rome was wont to bend its standards for the rich and prominent. Why, only a few years before, the Duchess of Marlborough had been granted an annulment, and she was the mother of two children by the Duke. In the smart salons of Mayfair, Waugh's annulment was thought to be assured.

The Vatican did not share this optimism. Waugh's petition did not even reach the curia for years. Perhaps there was some reluctance to grant to a recent convert that which had so often been denied to those born into the faith. Perhaps the Marlborough annulment had been too recent and too controversial. For whatever reason, Waugh's petition gathered dust. The clock ticked and nothing happened, except that each day Laura Herbert became one day older, and she was already surrounded by highly eligible suitors.

Waugh was desperate. He had to get that annulment. He was told that the church could not be hurried, but this was Evelyn Waugh with a Herbert bride in his sights. He could hurry the turning of the earth for such a prize.

Not even the Axis was out of bounds in his efforts to win church favor. He expressed public support for Mussolini and was one of the few English correspondents in Abyssinia who favored an Italian victory over its former colony. He believed that if Italian imperial expansion was frustrated by England

and other members of the League of Nations, Mussolini would be driven into an alliance with Hitler. (This soon occurred.) Since Nazi Germany was at that time threatening Catholic Austria, Waugh's views were warmly shared by the church. On his way back from Abyssinia, Waugh had a private interview in Rome with a very friendly Benito Mussolini. (We don't know whether he asked Il Duce to put in a good word with you-know-who a few blocks away.) Waugh wrote to another favorite correspondent, the famously beautiful Lady Diana Cooper, daughter of the tenth Duke of Rutland (well, the daughter of the Duchess of Rutland who was at the time married to the tenth Duke, who was a good sport about the whole thing), that his stock was rising with Laura's family because of "this lucky" war in Abyssinia in which he had publicly supported the Catholic side.

Laura's family, however, did not grant annulments. The church did. However, Waugh, as we have seen, was a relentless suitor. He soon published a biography titled *Edmund Campion: Jesuit and Martyr*, about a brilliant Jesuit priest who was hanged, drawn, and quartered in Elizabethan England, and beatified in the nineteenth century. Waugh dedicated all profits from this work to the rebuilding of Campion Hall, the Jesuit house at Oxford. The book was well received, particularly in the Catholic press, and Waugh was awarded the Hawthornden Prize, said to be England's highest literary honor.

Perhaps more impressive as a voucher of his faith was Waugh's completion of "the grimmest pilgrimage in Christendom," to Lough Derg, in County Donegal, Ireland, which included spending two nights in prayer on a small island in the middle of the lake, walking barefoot over sharp rocks, an all-night vigil, and almost nothing to eat or drink.

It was time well spent. On his return, badly in need of sustenance, he went immediately to his London club, the redoubtable St. James's, and found there a telegram from Rome announcing that his annulment had been granted.

Prayer, charity, and good connections may have helped, but it is hard to argue that Waugh's first marriage should not have been annulled. Both Evelyns had agreed at the outset not to have children, and had taken measures to ensure this. They were young when they were married, often separated, and soon parted. It really had not been much of a marriage at all.

So Waugh was free to marry Laura Herbert, if she would have him. As it turned out, she would. He had seen her often while waiting to hear from Rome, and she, too, had fallen in love. Her mother, Mary Herbert, daughter of the tenth Duke of Wemyss, while not enthusiastic, gradually became used to the idea.

The engagement was less equably received by other members of the bride's family. "I thought we'd heard the last of that young man," huffed Laura's aunt, Lady Victoria Herbert, who was an aunt of She-Evelyn as well.

The announcement in *The Times* had been scooped the previous day by Waugh's friend Tom Driberg, in the *Express*. He had been given this head start on the condition that he not mention Waugh's earlier marriage.

In April 1937, Laura Herbert married Evelyn Waugh. She was nineteen and he was thirty-one. Since her father was dead, she was given away by her fourteen-year-old brother, Auberon, who, in the car on the way to the church, literally sobbed and begged her not to marry someone so unworthy of their family. His tears were ignored.

The bride's grandmother Lady Vesey gave the couple a

generous wedding present of £4,000. This, plus some money of his own, enabled Evelyn to buy Piers Court, a splendid country home in the Cotswolds, a beautiful area in west central England. He filled it with books, art, servants, and, year by year, children. He had the Waugh and Herbert coats of arms placed above the front door.

He had married into the highest branches of the aristocracy. He was a country squire with an elegant estate. He had made it clear to Laura before their marriage that he would need physical separation from his family in order to write, and she honored this need. His best books were still ahead. When not writing he alternated between being lord of his manor and the center of the brightest circle in London. He would eventually upgrade his club from the St. James's to White's. He wined and dined and corresponded with the greatest names and quickest wits of his time.

He had climbed to the top of the hill.

CHAPTER 4

Love Finds Eric Blair

—

ERIC BLAIR WAS PERHAPS THE LEAST ELIGIBLE BACHelor in the British Isles, at least as far as eligible women were concerned. For him, an eligible woman was someone highly intelligent, well educated, good-looking, and sympathetic to his political views.

This list of requirements raised several problems. Even as late as the 1930s, there weren't many women in England who had been permitted the highest quality of education that was available to men. And, educated or not, it was difficult for any woman to be accepted in the workplace for any well-paying position. Women were expected to be supported by their husbands. Even women who would have preferred to support themselves knew this was nearly impossible, and so were forced to take a good, hard look at the prospects of any suitor. It did not take long to see that Blair's prospects were, like his appearance, grim.

He had not merely descended, as was his intention, to the bottom of the hill. He had willingly jumped, and the bottom was rock bottom. Soon after returning from Burma he moved to France, for a life of disgusting work and terrible poverty. He was always ill and often hungry. His clothes were shabby. He had given up a career in Burma that paid fairly well and would have ensured a comfortable retirement. Now he had no job at all, and he wasn't looking for one. He wanted to be a writer. He was absolutely certain of it.

The remarkable thing is that he had no doubts about his new career. There was, after all, so little evidence to support the notion that he was destined to be a writer. His early work was halting and clumsy. One young lady to whom he showed his first efforts thought they were "like a cow with a musket." An early Blair story began "Inside the park the crocuses were out." Unlike Waugh, whose wit and style were evident from the start, Blair had to teach himself to write, painfully at first, but steadily and tirelessly, until slowly, day by day, resolve began to be transformed into craft.

His persistence was admirable, but it didn't budge him from the bottom of the marriage prospect list. He was a writer who couldn't get anything published. He wrote two novels, but he destroyed one after his first rejection letter and later rewrote the other. He wrote short stories, too, and a good deal of journalism. But with the exception of a few essays published in small French literary journals, nothing he submitted made it into print.

And he had been robbed of all his savings. According to his published account of the incident, when he was living in Paris in 1929 a thief broke into several apartments in the building, and the robbery left him destitute. He gave a different account to a close friend: He had picked up what he called "a little trollop" in a café. She was beautiful, and he was crazy about her. She moved in with him. One day he came home and found her gone—along with all his money and everything he owned. He had only the few coins in his pocket. Hungry and desperate, he took a job as a dishwasher at a luxury hotel and then at a fashe like Oliver

return from
as published
not only the
the pseudo-
submitted to
which the
me.

book was
e had come
unknown
Days, but
first came
n's Daugh-
e reprinted
ost nothing
occasionally
ge income

oscurity, ill
attractive
gly, the in-
to Brenda
d him. He
to propos-

rty. (This
.) He co-
studying
d some of

is in what he described
is where incredibly ex-
He eventually used all
s and London, which is
lose weight.

r returned to England.
now it was time for
g his parents' house in
so as to be better able
dn't enjoy it; naturally

Square and spent other
perately associated with
rodden wretches in the
essed, how infrequently
ant and gray and sick he
g problem of never re-
company he sought. His
the hoboes knew imme-
rs could conceal Blair's
amps addressed him as
ny.

y for the poor old Blairs.
wed up he looked a little
of it. They should have
king in Kent. In London
g clean the old house in
e floors and cleaned the
crown a day (about sixty
llow lodgers called him
rel and Hardy; he *did* re-

semble the tall, thin Stan Laurel. (Waugh was mo
Hardy.)

More than five years had passed since Blair'
Burma before *Down and Out in Paris and London*
in January 1933 by Victor Gollancz, who named
book but the author. Gollancz helped Blair choos
nym "George Orwell" from a list that the autho
him. (Blair had recently been in Ipswich, throu
river Orwell runs.) He never legally changed his

He was almost thirty years old when that f
published. Waugh had been twenty-three, and fa
soon after. But the newly named Orwell remai
to the general public. He wrote a novel, *Burm*
couldn't find an English publisher and so the bc
out in America. He wrote another novel, *A Clergy*
ter, and was so unhappy with it that he never let
in his lifetime. He wrote all the time but earned a
from his efforts. He supplemented his income b
teaching and by working in a bookstore. His av
was less than £150 a year.

He did not permit his near poverty, shabbines
health, or stark appearance to inhibit his pursui
young women, though in many cases, not surpr
terest was primarily on his part. He propos
Salkeld, an actual clergyman's daughter, who rej
was often turned down by other women in respo
als of more temporary arrangements.

And then one evening Orwell actually gave
was roughly akin to Waugh becoming a coal n
hosted the event with his landlady in London. Sh
psychology at University College London and i

her fellow students. One of them was a young lady named Eileen O'Shaughnessy. She was never described as a great beauty, but her photographs show her to be very attractive indeed, and her abundant kindness, intelligence, and love of life are suggested even in a snapshot. Before the evening was over, Orwell had told his landlady that Eileen was the kind of girl he would like to marry.

She was one of the few women at that time to have earned an Oxford degree. She was bright and gifted and had studied under J.R.R. Tolkien, but since it was so difficult for a woman to obtain a well-paying job, Oxford graduate or not, she taught for a while, did clerical work, and eventually ran her own typing agency. When she met Blair she was studying for her master's degree. If Orwell felt by the end of their first evening together that he wanted to marry her, she undoubtedly had figured out just as quickly that he scarcely had a shilling to his name.

But she liked him. She saw at once his strengths and his flaws—he was a great artist and would always care more for his work than for her. She accepted that. She enjoyed being with him. She loved talking with him. Their courtship began.

They went horseback riding in the country. (Orwell, the former imperial policeman, rode well. At the same time, Evelyn Waugh was taking riding lessons so that he wouldn't be the only one at country weekends who was unable to join the hunt.) When Orwell proposed to Eileen, she turned him down at first because she didn't want to be a drain on his finances. She asked him to wait until she had earned her master's degree.

In the meantime, he had a project that would keep him fully occupied. Victor Gollancz had commissioned Orwell to go to the industrial north of England and report on the laborers' conditions there. This was at the height, or rather the depth, of the Depression. Times were bad even for those who still had jobs. There was near-starvation for those who did not. The north of England was a harsh and forbidding place marked by poverty and hopelessness. So this was, to Orwell, a dream assignment.

He spent several months in the north, visiting Manchester, Liverpool, and Sheffield. He went down into coal mines, despite his great height and weak lungs. He lived with the subjects of his study in their crowded and drafty homes. He shared their food. And yet they, too, to his chagrin, called him "Sir."

When he was through with his exhausting tour, he sat down to write a book about it.

Where he chose to sit down and write was scarcely more comfortable than the hovels he had just left. He went to the town of Wallington in Hertfordshire. Not really even a town, Wallington had fewer than one hundred inhabitants. Aside from very old, very damp, and very ugly houses, there were only a pub and a church. The place seemed isolated; no other villages were close, let alone a city of any size.

So what brought him there? It was The Stores. This was the name, so to speak, of the cottage in Wallington that had been inhabited by Eric Blair's Aunt Nellie. He took over her tenancy and moved into the tiny place. The only rational excuse for doing so was that the rent was very cheap—only seven shillings and sixpence a week (about $1.75 then).

There was a reason the rent was so low. The cottage dated from the early 1500s, and it was not charming, merely old. With no indoor plumbing, nor electricity, the house was simply two small rooms on the first floor and two tiny bedrooms just above. The stairway was unlighted, even by lamps.

It was called The Stores because it once had contained a

Little Eric Blair,
age three, the pudgy
offspring of empire.

The young but scrappy
Evelyn Waugh.

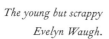

*Eric Blair fishing with friends in the "golden country,"
the loss of which he felt all his life.*

*The swimming pool at St. Cyprian's. Eric Blair's hatred of the school
(and a particular disgust for the pool) festered all his life.*

The house in Golders Green—of which Evelyn Waugh was ashamed—and his father, mother, and brother.

Richard Blair, Eric's father: the daily stroll of a retired civil servant who certainly looks like something lordlier.

Eric Blair (center) at Eton.

Evelyn Waugh visiting Oxford after having dropped out.

*The detested
C.R.M.F. Cruttwell,
whose taunting of
Waugh provoked a
lifetime of return fire.*

*The Police Training School at Mandalay, Burma.
Blair is standing third from left.*

The Bright Young
People: dawn after a
Mozart party, in which
the revelers take over a
jackhammer from the
few employed persons
in the picture.

Evelyn Gardner Waugh at a
costume party, hopefully one with
a circus theme.

Portrait of emerging author
Evelyn Waugh, by fashionable
artist Henry Lamb. Brian
Guinness paid for the painting,
so Waugh insisted on holding
a glass of his friend's
foamy product.

She-Evelyn and He-Evelyn
at a party (tropical theme) as
their marriage was ending.

Eileen O'Shaughnessy,
who became Mrs. Blair.

On the Aragon front in the Spanish Civil War.
Orwell is the tallest man in the picture,
and Eileen is crouched at his feet.

A Communist poster Orwell saw in
Barcelona during the Spanish Civil
War. It made quite an impression:
"If you want a picture of the future,
imagine a boot stamping on a human
face—forever." (From 1984.)

Laura Herbert with her sixteen-year-old brother, Auberon, who is not concealing his displeasure that she is about to marry Evelyn Waugh.

Top of the hill: The successful young author in front of his wedding present, Piers Court.

The Stores: the wretched home of the Blairs, in Wallington.

Waugh in his Royal Marines uniform.

"They also serve": Orwell and T. S. Eliot broadcasting to India in 1942.

Evelyn Waugh and Randolph Churchill in Croatia. Only one is smiling.

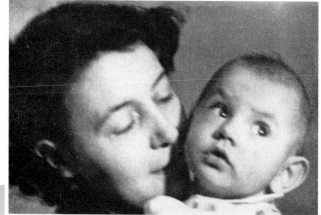

Eileen with newly adopted baby, Richard.

The long and lonely road to Barnhill, on Jura.

Orwell with Richard after Eileen's death.

Two great craftsmen at work.

The Waugh family at Piers Court.

Laura Waugh rushing (alone) to her wounded son's bedside.

In the foreground, Sonia Brownell, who married
George Orwell shortly before his death.

Waugh's perfect impersonation of the pompous country squire,
in front of his home, Combe Florey House. The sign on the pillar
reads NO ADMISSION ON BUSINESS.

shop, which Orwell reopened. It was a stretch even to call it a shop. Its stock was limited to the most rudimentary foodstuffs and a few household items. The space around the counter was eleven feet square. Access was through the cottage front door, which was four and a half feet high. (Orwell was six foot three, so the coal mine had been good practice.)

Though visiting friends, Etonians or not, found the little place deplorable, Blair seemed to think it was enchanting. Its extraordinary isolation made it a useful place to write a book, and he started at once to type away on his inspection of the north. He called his book *The Road to Wigan Pier.*

He was isolated but not alone, for Eileen joined him. She dropped out of school before receiving her master's degree and moved into the cottage in Wallington. That was infatuation. And even after seeing it, she stayed. That was true love.

They were married on June 9, 1936, just short of Orwell's thirty-third birthday. It was a small wedding. The guests consisted of Orwell's parents and sister, and Eileen's mother and her brother, Laurence, and his wife, Gwen. (Eileen worshipped her brother, a brilliant thoracic surgeon. She once said, "If we were at opposite sides of the world and I sent [Laurence] a telegram saying 'come at once' he would come. George would not do that. For his work comes before anything.")

The wedding took place in the small village church. Orwell, whose love of the time-honored traditions of the English people sometimes exceeded his exact knowledge of them, committed a small and rather endearing faux pas by attempting before the ceremony to carry Eileen over the threshold of the church. At the reception later (at the only other place it could possibly be held—the pub), Blair's mother and sister commiserated with the bride.

The couple settled into The Stores. Eileen prepared the meals, cleaned the cottage, stood behind the small counter waiting patiently to sell God-knows-what to God-knows-who (there is an account of children buying cheap candy), and listened to her husband type. The Orwells would keep the residence for ten years. This damp little cottage in nowhere was his Piers Court.

But they did, after some months, take a delayed honeymoon of sorts. It was called the Spanish Civil War.

At about the time of their wedding there was a general election in Spain. A Popular Front government came to power, very much to the left of and hostile to the established order, including the church. As is often the case in countries when the voters make this choice, the military staged a coup d'état, this one led by General Francisco Franco. But the elected government armed the workers—a remarkable step back then—and so instead of a successful coup the country was plunged into a ferocious civil war between the Republicans, who supported the elected government and its republic, and the Nationalists, led by Franco, who supported the church, the monarchy, the military, and business. It was not quite that simple, for there were divisions based on geography as well.

What is undisputed is that it was a real war, with trenches, artillery, bombing of cities, and terrible atrocities on both sides.

And it was, in a way, the out-of-town opening of World War II. Franco's army received considerable military support from Hitler and Mussolini. The Republicans were significantly aided by Stalin.

The democracies sent no weapons or support, and there was considerable division, particularly in the press, over which side to favor, but thousands of volunteers rushed to Spain to fight alongside the Republicans. (In America, the McCarthyites years later would condemn some of these volunteers as "premature anti-Fascists." This is exactly the sort of phrase that is now universally known as "Orwellian." One man can make a difference.)

George Orwell decided to go to Spain to fight against Franco, leaving Eileen to tend the shop and ensure that *The Road to Wigan Pier* was properly published. He intended to write about his experiences in Spain, and so described himself as a correspondent, though he was, in fact, a full-time soldier on the Republican side.

Traveling to Spain to fight, even as a volunteer, was not easy. You needed to be sponsored. Orwell's politics at this time were still unformed. He hated the class structure in England but at the same time believed strongly in tradition. He wanted to fight in Spain because the Republicans had been fairly elected, and Franco and his allies were like the bullies at St. Cyprian's. He surely did not see himself at a specific, let alone nuanced, spot on the political spectrum. Indeed, he first sought his traveling papers from the British Communist Party. They recognized where he stood better than he did and turned him down.

On arriving in Spain, Orwell joined up in Catalonia with the POUM (the Workers' Party of Marxist Unification), which was left-wing but anti-Stalin. (The Stalinists referred to POUM members as Trotskyites.) Most of the Spanish soldiers with whom he fought were young and uneducated. Orwell, who had received military training at Eton, and spent five years in the Imperial Police, was given a small leadership role, but his influence was limited by the troops' indifference to any form of discipline.

Orwell did fight, though, bravely and tirelessly. He was in

his thirties, his health had always been bad, and life in the trenches made it worse, but he never complained. He fought, and he killed.

Eileen eventually came to Spain to be with him. She could get no closer than a hotel in Barcelona, but he was able to join her often.

In Barcelona Orwell observed hostilities quite different from those at the front. He saw many funeral processions, though the deceased had not been killed in battle. They had been assassinated—by those ostensibly on the same side. The communists were trying to take over the Republican government. They accused the POUM of being fascists. They widely circulated a cartoon to illustrate this charge, showing a person wearing a mask with a hammer and sickle on it. But when the mask was pulled off, a swastika was exposed for all the world to see. Some of Orwell's friends in Spain had disappeared; others were in jail or had been murdered. An English passport was no protection for either of the Blairs. It certainly had not saved the lives of other victims of the communists.

Orwell resolved to leave soon, but first he returned to the front. And while there he was severely wounded. It was largely his own fault. He had been warned not to stand in the trenches, as they had been dug for the concealment of Spanish soldiers, who generally were much shorter than he was. But disregarding danger, Orwell stood up at dawn one day to light a cigarette and was immediately shot through the throat by a fascist sniper. The bullet just missed his carotid artery, which would have meant swift death. He was still badly wounded and unable to speak. (His voice was never the same again.) He was treated in the field, bounced over bumpy roads in a crowded ambulance, and eventually ended up in a field hospital in the nearby town of Lérida.

Eileen rushed from Barcelona to be at his side. She arranged for him to be transferred to a sanatorium near Barcelona. Fortunately for him (or perhaps through Eileen's foresight) it was run by the POUM. This significant fact, as well as her continual care, may well have saved his life.

Orwell slowly recovered but was certified as medically unfit. He and Eileen prepared to return to England, but he needed a medical discharge certificate from an officer at the front, lest he be thought a deserter. So, though very weak, he returned to the battlefield in order to get the official papers.

As it turned out, the front was the safest place for him to be. While he had been recuperating, the communists had begun aggressively to liquidate the POUM. During Orwell's trip to the front, the POUM was declared illegal and its officers arrested. The sanatorium where Orwell had stayed was raided.

When Orwell returned to Barcelona with his discharge papers, he went into the Hotel Continental, where Eileen was staying. He found her sitting in the lounge. Calmly, she got up, smiled, and came over to him. She put her arm around his neck. It seemed such an affectionate and natural greeting. But when she leaned over, her lips by his ear, she hissed, "Get out!" That was all. Though puzzled and confused, he understood the fear in her eyes and so let her lead him out into the street. There they encountered a Frenchman they knew. He beseeched them to leave quickly before the police arrived at the hotel.

Eileen told him that two days earlier six plainclothes police had invaded her room. They had taken Orwell's diary and other papers, but Eileen had managed to conceal his passport. A warrant had been issued for the arrest of both Eric and Eileen Blair. The police probably let her stay in the hotel so that when Orwell returned they could get them both. The couple had been condemned as Trotskyites, agents of the POUM, fascists. If caught now, they would be killed.

They decided it was safer to separate. They would meet at the British consulate the next day. Blair spent the night sleeping in the ruins of a bombed-out church.

They met at the consulate, but even when their passports were in order Orwell delayed their own flight by trying to help others escape, too. He visited a friend, Georges Kopp, in the Barcelona jail, a brave but foolhardy move, and when Kopp said he needed some papers from the War Department, Orwell went there in search of the documents. He was recognized and was lucky to leave the building alive. (It was like *Dr. Strangelove*. "You can't shoot anyone here. This is the War Department.") He slept amid tall grass that night. The next day, they visited Kopp in jail again! The gentle English, accustomed, even in foreign lands, to going where they wished, still did not fully comprehend that a new age was dawning, in which war was not limited to soldiers on battlefields but included everyone, everywhere.

But the Orwells knew they had to get out, fast. They bought tickets for an evening train to France, but when they arrived at the station found that it had left early. They spent the night in hiding and took a morning train. When they reached the French border their passports were carefully examined on the Spanish side by officials whose orders now came from the communists. But the call for their arrest had not yet reached the border guards. Mr. and Mrs. Blair did their best to act like English tourists. After what must have seemed an eternity, they were allowed to cross over into France, and soon after that were back in England.

The Spanish Civil War was the great altering event in the life of Eric Blair. It was in Spain, not earlier when he assumed a pen name, that he really became George Orwell.

Until he had witnessed the Spanish Civil War firsthand, he had been limited by his Englishness. The essential decency and common sense of the British people had cushioned his rage at the rigid class structure that was part of England's heritage as well. The worst thing he could imagine was St. Cyprian's—bullies tormenting their classmates for not being born to wealth. And he hated unearned privilege for the few when so many were so poor. But for him this concentration of power was just a national extension of St. Cyprian's. For years social injustice had been the furthest extension of evil he could see, and it had been enough to direct his life.

But in Spain he saw there was even more to fear and to fight against. The future—and the foreign armers of the sniper who shot him, Mussolini and Hitler, were widely assumed to be the future—was something far beyond what he had fought against before. It wasn't just *injustice* any longer. That was an English word, and the cure for the problem was to make things more just—to have faith in Dickens and Wells and Shaw and seminars.

Mussolini coined a new word for the new world: totalitarianism. Precisely. This was not mere injustice, a singular flaw in a generally favorable framework—this was *total*. It was a whole new framework, a new reality. It was the complete control of people's minds and the death of those who resisted.

While in Spain, Orwell received the English newspapers. What he read was completely different from what he saw all

around him. He realized with great shock that the Irish philosopher Bishop Berkeley was right in that the only reality is what
people *perceive* to be reality. If you and your friends are naïve
English liberals fighting for democracy against Franco, and the
newspapers, the government, and *history* says that instead you
are a fascist, then even though you *know* you're not a fascist,
you still are one—because the new reality is total. What's in
your head can't be true because it isn't in anyone else's head—
and it isn't in your head either because you will be brainwashed
or shot. Orwell just barely escaped being shot, and many of his
friends and fellow volunteers did not.

So now Orwell knew. He knew that this new thing, totalitarianism, was bent on destroying objective reality, and that this
threat was far more fearsome than poison gas or bombs. The
book that says this more powerfully than any other, *1984,* which
was written in 1948, was born in Catalonia in 1937. Orwell now
knew what the Modern Age would bring, and for the rest of his
life he was the bravest and strongest warrior against it.

He fought with his typewriter. He spent much of his time in
Wallington, at The Stores, clacking away, with Eileen back behind the counter, making meals and tending to her husband's
health and needs. Today it seems like a terribly subservient
role, but it was her free and informed choice. Though he took
her for granted, and gave her not even fidelity, it is difficult to
see how Orwell could have carried on without her, for she
loved him, and she nurtured him and his work. She saw fully,
before anyone else—before he himself saw it—the full scope of
his art and his genius. And she knew as well as he the nature of
the enemy whose defeat was his destiny. She also had found that
enemy in Spain, and she fought it, too, by adding her quiet
strength to his own. She did so until the day she died.

CHAPTER 5

The Waugh to End All Waughs

—

WHEN THE ENGLISH THINK ABOUT SEPTEMBER 1, 1939, it is in much the same way that Americans remember December 7, 1941. You don't have to ask what happened on that date. The war began. Everyone who was around then remembered for the rest of their lives what they had been doing when they heard the news.

On the first day of September 1939, Evelyn Waugh was one of the very few men of means in Great Britain who did not own a radio. The wireless, as it was then called, would have disturbed the pastoral tranquillity of Piers Court, his lovingly adorned Georgian manor house on forty-one acres in Gloucestershire. There he saw only those he chose to see. His small world was ordered exactly as he wanted it.

But on occasion it was necessary to leave that sheltered world, however brief the mission. So on September 1, Waugh went to the local vicarage to borrow some folding chairs for a tea party. The vicar did own a wireless, and had just learned from it that Germany had begun bombing Poland. Everyone knew at once that this meant war. Many had been expecting it for months.

Waugh had seen it coming much earlier than that. In *Vile Bodies*, published in 1930, his hero and heroine are enjoying a blissful weekend in a country manor house with no wireless. The local rector rushes over to give them the astonishing news he has just heard on his own wireless. "The most terrible and unexpected thing . . . War has been declared." While it took Prime Minister Neville Chamberlain until September 3 to actually broadcast that a state of war existed, the confluence of Waugh's tale with history as it unfolded a decade later is striking. *Vile Bodies* ends on a battlefield of a continent almost totally leveled by hideous modern weaponry. Waugh had known in his heart as far back as the 1920s, amid all those dances, those feverish parties, what would finally come with the dawn. And when it did come, on September 1, 1939, he dutifully recorded the rector's announcement in his diary, and then ended that day's entry by calmly noting, "Today Evans finished the new arrangements of panels in the library. The west wall is now symmetrical and, with the George III portrait, looks absolutely splendid." So much for the outside world.

George Orwell was also prescient about the war. He saw what was coming as early as 1931, he wrote in his wartime diary, and his vision was as accurate as Waugh's. "The future must be catastrophic," he had seen.

Artists foresee what statesmen do not. A shockingly unprepared England rushed to be ready for battle. It was clear now not only that war had come, but that the price of war for England, win or lose (and a great many English thought that their side would lose), would be the death of their sons and brothers in even greater numbers than in the ghastly carnage a generation earlier.

In this regard, the safest year for a boy to be born in England was probably 1903. It would have left him too young to be slaughtered in World War I, and just a little too old for active service in World War II. Technically, at the start of the war, conscription went up to age forty-one, but this was not fully implemented, and the likelihood of passing the physical examination was much reduced for those nearing forty. So was the expectation of active service. Orwell and Waugh both had been born in 1903, and many Englishmen of the same age considered themselves lucky indeed to have arrived in life in such a convenient year.

But neither Orwell nor Waugh felt himself lucky at all. They both *wanted* to fight for their country against the Nazis, who, among so many other failings, embodied for them the Modern Age. They saw military service in this war as the highest possible moral obligation. Both, because of age and talent, were logical choices for the Ministry of Information or some other government agency. But they didn't want to produce propaganda; they wanted active duty. "There is a symbolic difference between fighting as a soldier and serving as a civilian, even if the civilian is more valuable," Waugh told his diary.

But the army didn't want them. They were, after all, among the least probable warriors in the land. Aside from the fact that they were too old (thirty-six at the outbreak of war), there were other factors to discourage even the most desperate recruiter. In Waugh's case, there was a lifetime of rich food and endless drink, the effects of which were unmistakable. The lifting of glasses had constituted his only habitual exercise, leaving merely an elbow likely to be approved for active duty. While psychological testing for officers then was minimal at best, Waugh's anarchic bellicosity, his savage whims, his disdain for authority, his penchant for astounding strangers through hopping in and out of his own fantasy world, together could have disqualified him even from consideration for the rigors of command.

And Orwell, physically at least, was in far worse shape. His health had been bad for a long time and was steadily growing worse. His lungs were terribly weak; he probably was already suffering from tuberculosis. He looked much older than he was. It was exhausting for him to walk even a few blocks. Military service of any kind seemed completely out of the question. The very sight of him would have made an army physical pointless. He would have been turned away at the door.

Yet both men did manage to serve, each in his own way.

At the outbreak of the war, Waugh wrote in his diary that he wanted to enlist as a private. It was a noble sentiment—the sybarite marching shoulder to shoulder with the yeoman—and no doubt putting these words on paper filled their author with a warm and genuine glow.

But as it turned out, Waugh entered the service as an officer. This was less a betrayal of his original resolve than a subsequent concession to reality. He would never have been accepted as an enlisted man. His only hope of joining up was through pulling strings, and the strings pulled by his crowd were attached only to the epaulets of officers. So that was the route he pursued. It took some doing, but compared to his three protracted efforts—two of them successful—to snare Herbert brides, landing a commission was something of a cinch. He did, after all, know a great many influential people. The problem was that they also knew him. Even so, he was nothing if not persistent, and his process soon came to resemble the application for admission to the best clubs.

Waugh now knew everyone whom he wanted to know. He had been a famous author for ten years. He had married into the high aristocracy. He was a clubman. He was not quite yet a member of White's, then and now the most exclusive of London clubs, but he soon would be, and in the meantime he was welcomed there as a guest by many friends. For an author of middle-class antecedents to seek membership in White's was an assault more hazardous than the upcoming Allied raid on Dieppe. Compared to this, obtaining a commission was relatively easy, especially if one had access to White's, or to Waugh's own club, the St. James's, whose bars were crowded with admirals and government ministers. Waugh went into full attack mode.

He had an interview at the Admiralty with, of all people, Ian Fleming, who seems to have been more shaken than stirred by the encounter, since Waugh left empty-handed. But unbowed. Other meetings were arranged. The glasses were refilled at White's and the St. James's. Friends spoke to friends.

And at last Waugh was given a commission as a second lieutenant in the Royal Marines. This achievement is even more remarkable when one learns that Waugh failed his physical examination for military service. The doctor couldn't help remarking on his "middle-aged spread," and Waugh's efforts to cheat on his eye exam proved unsuccessful.

Nonetheless, the Marines took him. He had been sent back to the Admiralty with a note reporting the flunked physical. The note was sealed, but Waugh, being Waugh, opened it in the cab and then wondered whether there was any use even in going to the Admiralty. He need not have worried. There was. "A colonel in khaki greeted me in the most affable way, apologized for keeping me waiting, and gradually it dawned on me that I was being accepted. He said 'The doctors do not think much of your eyesight. Can you read that?', pointing to a large advertisement across the street. I could. 'Anyway most of your work will be in the dark.' " Waugh was given a choice of assignments and picked the Marine Infantry in the hope of taking part in raids on enemy territory.

Obviously, the colonel had been determined to approve Waugh for active service. Total blindness or the absence of a limb probably would not have mattered. Waugh's acceptance was undoubtedly due to his two sponsors. The first was Winston Churchill—not quite yet prime minister but First Lord of the Admiralty, which, under the circumstances, was even better. The second was Brendan Bracken, Churchill's right-hand man. When Churchill *did* move into Number 10 Downing Street, Bracken moved in with him. By 1941 he was the minister of information. The word "network" then meant a way of catching lobsters, but in its contemporary usage of getting to know everyone who might be helpful, Waugh was clearly in a class of his own.

On hearing that the famous author Evelyn Waugh had sought and achieved active duty, the saintly Orwell for once was jealous. "Why can't someone on the Left do something like that?" he wrote to a friend. Actually, of course, many on the left did sign up, too, though perhaps with less assistance than Waugh received. Others in the literary community fled to America, earning the undying contempt of both Orwell and Waugh. The two most celebrated émigrés were W. H. Auden and Christopher Isherwood. For Waugh, these writers became the new Cruttwells, though, English libel laws being what they were, he changed their names to Parsnip and Pimpernel when he ridiculed them in print.

Though few would have predicted it, Waugh was a very good marine, at least in combat. He was brave and tireless. He suffered heat and hunger and prolonged lack of sleep without complaint. He was calm and resourceful under fire. He was promoted to captain.

Away from combat, he was much like his old self, often rude and sarcastic. Those under his command, who suffered and bitterly resented his verbal abuse, were likely unaware that he was just as rude to his own commanding officers. He didn't care who he insulted, his singular democratic trait.

This could offer little comfort to his victims in the ranks. Many hated Captain Waugh. They wanted to kill him. This is not a metaphor: When Waugh was denied more active duty by a senior officer who feared he might be shot, a friend suggested helpfully, "That's a chance we all must take."

"I wasn't talking about the enemy," replied the officer. Indeed, a night guard was stationed to protect the tent of the sleeping Captain Waugh—and this was when he was still in England!

Whatever the reason, Waugh was clearly kept from active duty. After serving with great valor and fortitude in the disastrous Crete campaign, where the British forces were routed by a smaller number of Germans, he went back to England to wait for orders that never came. He was disconsolate. He wanted desperately to be in the thick of battle instead of sitting in his bespoke uniform in White's Club, of which he had now become a member, drinking in vain for an assignment.

He had enough time on leave to write *Brideshead Revisited*, which he considered his masterwork, but he still would have preferred to be sent into battle.

Why was he not? He believed he was kept from command because of his political views. In the 1930s he had written favorably of both Franco and Mussolini (though he was always anti-

Nazi). Given that this was, after all, a war against Fascism, he felt his earlier screeds were keeping him not only from further promotion but from more active service as well. And indeed, there is evidence that higher-ups vetoed his requests. Brendan Bracken, who had become his champion string puller in England, was thought to have turned against his protégé, who was badly hurt on hearing this. Waugh, despite intense devotion to his faith, was congenitally indisposed to turning the other cheek. He was very much an eye-for-an-eye man, and then some. So Brendan Bracken in *Brideshead Revisited* became Rex Mottram, "a tiny part of a human being posing as the whole thing." However satisfying this small act of revenge may have been to Waugh, it did nothing to further his assignment to a foreign battlefield.

And then, as if from the God to whom he daily prayed, the summons came. Major Randolph Churchill needed a second in command for a mission of great danger and strategic importance in Croatia. His choice was Captain Evelyn Waugh.

Britain had made it a high war priority to tie up German soldiers through stiff resistance in the Balkans. Not many troops were available for this purpose, and so the plan was to back and supply local guerrillas. But *which* local guerrillas? This being the Balkans, there were many rival factions, and some were busy fighting one another. It had finally been decided to back the Partisans, whose leader was said to be a man named Tito. In order to ensure Tito's alliance, it was important that he knew he enjoyed strong British support. Accordingly, no less than the prime minister's only son had been selected to head this mission. He was permitted to name his own deputy; in July 1944 he did so.

Elated, Waugh accepted with alacrity. The two had long been friends. This is not surprising, given that they inhabited the same small mountaintop in the English social landscape. Though Waugh had outclimbed Tenzing to arrive there, Churchill, of course, had been born to those heights. His great-grandfather was the Duke of Marlborough. Randolph Churchill not only was an aristocrat, he was also confident, commanding, and, at least in his youth, a model of physical perfection.

But he had not lived up to this early promise. Even in a circle highly tolerant of such inclinations, he was notorious for drinking, philandering, gambling, rudeness, brawling, and conceit. When he proposed to Pamela Digby, her friends begged her to decline. They were right. It was a union that in affection and fidelity made Evelyn Waugh's first marriage seem like that of Victoria and Albert. While Randolph was serving in the army overseas, Pamela had an affair with (among others) Franklin Roosevelt's emissary in London, Averell Harriman. Randolph angrily believed his father had known of this liaison and had tolerated it because of his need to influence FDR. Many years and adventures later, Pamela married Harriman and eventually became the American ambassador to France. In a recent biography of her extraordinary life there is a full-page picture of a remarkable-looking young man with the single pathetic caption "Alcohol robbed Randolph Churchill of his looks, wives and friends, but as a youth he was astonishingly handsome."

Perhaps alcohol was not the only cause of his arrested promise. It is difficult to be the only son of a great man. Randolph Churchill was precocious as a youth; he had charm and wit, a quick mind, a fluent pen, and infectious enthusiasm. But these could not compare to the same qualities in his father. "Beneath the mighty oak, no saplings grow," was an adage that Randolph himself used to quote. He smiled when he said it, but he said it often.

Though Waugh's promise had been fulfilled, he was, of course, not free of imperfection, either. His reputation in polite company was in fact similar to Churchill's. Excessive drink and outrageous behavior were common to them both, as was the absolute assurance with which each chose to dumbfound the world. In the officers' mess as well as in Mayfair, the timid and the civil fled at their approach.

Since each man was always on stage, and world-class hams are loath to share the spotlight, we may ask why these two teamed up. The most honest answer appears in Waugh's diary: "No one else would have chosen me, nor would anyone else have accepted him." But just to make sure of snaring him, Churchill told Waugh he was needed to heal the great schism between the Catholic and Orthodox churches in Croatia. That this wafer was swallowed whole shows that it takes one great con man to con another.

At first, things went swimmingly. Waugh was in a temporary haze of good fellowship, overseeing action at last, and seemingly in the service of the church as well. Much of his past association with Churchill was warmly remembered. They had been the two godfathers at the christening of Diana and Bryan Guinness's son. They had attended many of the same parties. In the army, they had been billeted near each other in Scotland and had shared a cabin on a transport ship to Egypt. Now the two became closer than ever. In fact, Waugh dedicated *Put Out More Flags* to Randolph Churchill. (Waugh wrote this small masterpiece aboard a troopship.) The Churchill dedication suggests a warmth of feeling that may not have been the exclusive motive for its inclusion. This was the same time that Waugh was up for membership in White's, and Waugh's subsequent admission was surprising to many. The name "Churchill" was particularly golden just then. We do not know whether the dedication tipped the balance in favor of Waugh's admission. If so, it was no more cunning a ploy than suggesting that the Croatian expedition had a holy purpose. The two men really did have much in common.

So, peaceably at first, the warriors embarked for Croatia. They stopped on the way in Algiers, staying at the British Embassy with Duff and Diana Cooper. The other guests included Bloggs Baldwin (son of former prime minister Stanley Baldwin), Mrs. Ernest Hemingway, and Baron Victor Rothschild. (The war, for their set, was a change in scene, not cast.) "I should think Randolph must go through two bottles of gin a day," the hostess complained.

Then they traveled to the island of Vis off Croatia's Dalmatian coast, where there was a British garrison, for the purpose of meeting Marshal Josip Broz Tito, the partisan leader the British were trying to win over. The encounter was not propitious.

Waugh was a subtle and creative bully. He knew instinctively and with enormous skill exactly how to drive other people mad. His favorite weapon, the deadliest in his arsenal, was to concoct a story that clearly was not true and then to stick to that story tenaciously, regardless of the facts or expositions of others, to the point where each repetition of this chimera, like the Chinese water torture, caused increased agony to his wildly frustrated audience.

A very good example of this is contained in *Brideshead Revisited*, which he had finished just shortly before embarking for

Croatia. Its narrator, Charles Ryder, has to put up with a father who played exactly the same game Waugh perfected in real life. Ryder invites to dinner at his father's London home an Oxford classmate, Jorkins, as obviously English as one could be:

> My father was master of the situation. He had made a little fantasy for himself, that Jorkins should be an American, and throughout the evening he played a delicate, one-sided parlour-game with him, explaining any peculiarly English terms that occurred in the conversation, translating pounds into dollars, and courteously deferring to him with such phrases as "Of course, by *your* standards . . . "; "All this must seem very parochial to Mr. Jorkins"; "In the vast spaces to which *you* are accustomed . . ." so that my guest was left with the vague sense that there was a misconception somewhere as to his identity, which he never got a chance of explaining. Again and again during dinner he sought my father's eye, thinking to read there the simple statement that this form of address was an elaborate joke, but met instead a look of such mild benignity that he was left baffled.

Waugh played his favorite game even more outrageously in life than in print. So on receiving his orders to journey to Croatia and win over Tito, Waugh summoned all his powers and finally went over the top. Earlier in the war, when Tito's name was first becoming known to the British, his identity remained vague. Some questioned whether he existed at all. Someone jokingly suggested that perhaps Tito was a woman. Waugh overheard this and was instantly inspired—it was like Cruttwell first mentioning dogs. He had a new theme, and he never let go. During all the London briefings about Croatia and Tito, Waugh kept asking when he would get to meet "her." Puzzled looks did not deter him; quite the contrary. Nor did the fact that on arriving on Vis he was taken to the beach and introduced to the strapping Tito, who was wearing only a close-fitting bathing suit. "Ask Captain Waugh," said the well-informed marshal, "why he thinks I am a woman." Others would have dissembled, but the Partisan had met his match. "Tito like Lesbian," Waugh wrote in his diary that evening.

Thereafter, he referred to the Yugoslav leader only as "Aunty." He certainly seemed to believe what he was saying, though with Waugh one never could tell. Later, when another officer remarked on how tiresome the marshal was being, Waugh replied, "I think she has come to a rather difficult age for women." Exasperated, the officer said, "For God's sake stop this nonsense, Evelyn. Everyone knows that he's a man and a good looking one at that." But Waugh merely shrugged and said, "Her face is pretty, but her legs are *very* thick." As late as 1953, when Tito, now head of state, visited London, Waugh wrote, "The politicians must be heartily sorry they imported the wench."

After encountering Tito, Evelyn and Randolph had gone to Bari, in the southeastern coast of Italy, and then headed for Croatia. They almost didn't make it. Their plane, on approaching the runway late at night, burst into flames and crashed. Of the nineteen people on board, ten were killed. Waugh was badly burned, and Churchill was hurt in both knees. They were flown to a hospital at Bari.

This was the first time they were truly confined together. Ominously, the Waugh diary suggests that the honeymoon was starting to end: "Randolph in hospital like 'the man who came

to dinner', drinking, attacking the night nurse, wanting everyone's medicine and all treatment, dictating letters, plastering
the hospital with American propaganda. . . . Soon he left for
Algiers and I found things more restful."

After two months of recuperation, they landed at last safely
in Croatia and set up headquarters in the town of Topusko. The
two officers shared a four-room house which, in local tribute to
the Downing Street connection, contained the only indoor
privy in the region. Topusko, now abandoned, had been a spa
town, and the therapeutic baths were still working. Waugh used
them every day.

There was little else to do. Essentially they were military
ambassadors of the British to the Partisans. Their goal was to
win the allegiance of a group of communists who would turn
their backs on the West as soon as the war was over, as Waugh
correctly prophesied. Tito did manage to become relatively independent of the Soviet Union; God only knows whether this
was despite or because of the Churchill/Waugh efforts on behalf of Great Britain. The basic British propaganda technique
was to display the son of their prime minister as frequently as
possible. Other than launching germ warfare, it is difficult to
imagine a less-effective means of winning over a populace.
Randolph was almost continuously drunk, and as ambassador
either comatose or belligerent. Not much work was done.

But numerous banquets were attended. Waugh, who bored
easily, found these interminable, and not without cause. One
dinner ended at 4 a.m. "The entertainment consisted of rousing
choruses in Russian, Yugoslav, and a language said to be English; a propaganda playlet from the Russian about a boy getting a medal from the state school; a dialogue between Hitler
and Reaction, played by a kind of witch; and a play about a

cowardly soldier who becomes brave by shooting a German. My Communist neighbor said, 'You see in spite of war we have the arts.' "

But tedious programs were nothing compared to Randolph Churchill, whose constant presence was driving Waugh mad. Waugh's diary is particularly full at this period, presumably because if he stopped writing and left his bedroom he would encounter Randolph. The pages grow more venomous: "Randolph, with ostrich-cunning, stayed in bed hoping to give the impression that he had been ill, not drunk, the night before." (The phrase, "ostrich-cunning," is purest Waugh: a sharp and unexpected metaphor.)

But it was more than drunkenness, however spectacular, that really bothered Waugh. There was the constant barrage of talk, the bellicosity, the endless harebrained schemes (trying to win over a commissar by reading to him from Macaulay on Warren Hastings), the frenetic and pointless puttering, the noise, the mess, the *incessancy* of Churchill that prevented Waugh from his own work. "I should like to start writing a novel but have not the opportunity unless I can persuade Randolph to go to Belgrade." Waugh needed solitude, and he was living with the last person in the world to provide it. "The facts are that he is a bore—with no intellectual invention or agility. He has a childlike retentive memory and repetition takes the place of thought. . . . He is not a good companion for a long period."

And there was something even worse. Randolph Churchill was a bully, and he tried to bully Waugh. "He is simply a flabby bully who rejoices in blustering and shouting down anyone weaker than himself and starts squealing as soon as he meets anyone as strong. In words he can understand, he can dish it out but he can't take it."

One constant in Waugh's life was his success at outbullying bullies. Churchill, of course, was a major challenge; among other things, he was Waugh's commanding officer. But basically he was a weak man, and now he was faced with a foe of iron will and demonic cunning. Waugh saw at once that no one could best Churchill through worse behavior—that was not possible—and so he transformed himself into the granite god of rectitude. He stopped drinking. He spoke quietly. He endured tirades in stony silence. He made it clear that *he* was the aristocrat and Churchill the savage. He saw that his aplomb drove Churchill wild, and so he polished the role daily until he reached perfection.

They were no longer quite alone in Tobusko. They had been joined by an old friend of both. Major Freddie Birkenhead, the Earl of Birkenhead, had been Lord in Waiting to the king before the war. He had known Randolph Churchill at Eton, and their families gathered annually at Blenheim Palace. He was just the sort of man whom Waugh would want to get to know, and therefore Waugh had. In later years, Birkenhead was a prolific biographer and has left a remarkable record of the Croatian farce that he joined in the second act.

He had much to describe, right from the start. When Birkenhead first arrived late one evening at the cottage in Tobusko,

> On the threshold, his arms spread wide in ecstatic welcome, stood Randolph. He greeted me with manic affection and shouts of joy, which would have been touching if one had not known from long experience how capricious his favor was. . . . I had the perhaps un-

worthy suspicion that the warmth of his greeting owed much to the rigors of his enforced confinement with Evelyn.

As we were talking, Evelyn, a demure figure in a brown woolen dressing-gown, joined us, summoned by Randolph's raucous bellows. "There he is!" roared the Mission Commander—"there's the little fellow in his camel-hair dressing-gown! Look at him standing there!" Evelyn directed on him a stare cold and hostile as the Arctic Ocean, and remarked with poisonous restraint: "You've got very drunk tonight. Don't send any more signals."

Both were short but sturdy, and as I watched them standing there in angry and ridiculous confrontation I was reminded of a pair of belligerent robins.

They came to seem more like hawks. It was not so bad during the day, but after sundown they were all trapped together in the cottage. One evening, as Birkenhead and Waugh were discussing literature, Churchill attempted to join the conversation. He referred to his father's epic *Life of Marlborough,* and asked Waugh whether he considered it a great work. Wrote Birkenhead:

He received the dustiest of answers: "As history," Evelyn replied with unattractive vigor, "it is beneath contempt, the special pleading of a defense lawyer. As literature it is worthless. It is written in a sham Augustan prose which could only have been achieved by a man who thought always in terms of public speech. . . ."

Randolph . . . remarked angrily to me: "Have you ever noticed that it is always the people who are most religious who are most mean and cruel?" . . . Evelyn replied, not only without rancor but almost with vivacity: "But my dear Randolph, you have no idea what I should be like if I wasn't."

The courtly Birkenhead stood transfixed as the two combatants went at it every day. But what he saw as battles were merely skirmishes. The decisive confrontation was yet to come. Birkenhead was roused from his sleep one night by Churchill, "his face transfigured by that mingled excitement and rage that so often possessed him at the approach of danger. 'Get up you fool,' he shouted: 'The Germans are over and they're trying to get me. They've got this house pinpointed—pinpointed I tell you!' "

The two men ran outside and discovered that Churchill was quite right. The Germans *were* trying to kill him. They'd heard that the son of their archenemy was stationed in Topusko, and a number of Luftwaffe planes were trying to bomb the cottage. Birkenhead and Churchill rushed to a nearby trench and dived in.

The enemy, having failed to flatten the house, turned and made a low run on the position which they next sprayed with machine-gun fire. As we had no anti-aircraft weapons, we could not respond, and were fortunate to avoid casualties. In the middle of this attack, the small figure of Evelyn, somehow overlooked, emerged from the Mission clad in a white duffle-coat which might have been designed to attract fire, and which gleamed in leprous prominence in the dawn. At this sight, Randolph's face, empurpled with rage, appeared over the trench and in tones verging on hysteria he screamed: "You bloody little swine, take off that coat! TAKE OFF THAT FUCKING COAT! It's an order! It's a military order!" Evelyn did not seem to regard even this dire threat as binding and without removing the coat lowered himself with leisurely dignity in to the trench among the bullets, pausing only on his way to remark to Randolph: "I'll tell you what I think of your repulsive manners when the bombardment is over."

They survived the attack, but the next day barely spoke. An icy silence reigned within the cottage.

"But Randolph soon began to yearn for a *détente* . . . and drawing Evelyn aside, apologized if his manners had been abrupt on the day of the attack, reminding him that as the Mission Commander he was responsible for the safety of all its members. Evelyn replied: 'My dear Randolph, it wasn't your manners I was complaining of: it was your cowardice.' "

That did it. Coventry Cathedral now had been leveled, and so Churchill started looking for his Dresden to bomb in response. He vowed to find a fitting revenge. Scheme after scheme was rejected as too subtle, but after much thought he finally had it. He played his best card, which was that of commanding officer. He issued a military order to Waugh to attend and take part in the celebration of a ghastly group called "The League of Anti-Fascist Women," and to join with them in their vivid national dance. Birkenhead went along and noted with horror, "These unsexed creatures, ferocious in appearance, were clad in battledress and wore girdles of live Mills Bombs round their waists, which jogged up and down when they moved." And of course they did more than just move. They danced. Violently, and without stop. They danced with Evelyn. That was the whole idea behind Major Churchill's order. The terrified writer was grasped and hugged and whisked around the earthen dance floor by Amazons wearing live grenades, against which he was smothered. Though he may have prayed for death, it did not occur.

The counterattack successful, Churchill was restored to his habitual manic good humor. He became more voluble than ever. This was a serious problem, for the galley proofs of *Brideshead Revisited* had miraculously arrived in Topusko (well, not so miraculously—they were sent via 10 Downing Street) and Waugh needed peace and quiet to make revisions. By this time Birkenhead, too, had developed a craving for solitude: "The intense relief of their uneasy truce caused Randolph to talk more than at any time since our arrival, and his appalling garrulity preyed to such an extent on our nerves that we decided at all cost that he must be silenced."

Birkenhead proposed a solution. He had brought with him a large family Bible. He and Waugh bet Churchill £100 that he could not read this massive volume in a fortnight and then answer questions about it. Churchill loved a wager—as they both knew—and jumped at this one. He took the Bible and left the room. Waugh and Birkenhead sighed with pleasure. Peace at last had blessed Topusko.

Or so they thought. As it turned out, Randolph was less absorbed in the Bible than stimulated by it. They had counted neither on his capacity for amazement nor on the astonishing fact that he was reading this work for the first time. This was all new to him—and each battle, sin, or exodus opened a spigot of excited commentary. Years later, Birkenhead wrote:

> Randolph's behavior had never been conspicuous for moral rectitude, but he now showed a shocked and uncharacteristic moral indignation at the turpitude of the Old Testament God, which gave him a further and ample field for comment. How well I remember that unquenchable eloquence, those ribald ecstasies—the premonitory rumbling, the rich eighteenth-century chuckles over salacious passages, the sudden explosions of moral outrage, of which, "Christ, God is a shit!" lingers particularly in the mind. The pace at which he covered the ground merely deepened our dejection, and Evelyn made a gesture of despair. Randolph appeared strangely ignorant of the Bible, which came to him therefore with a delicious freshness: "Why was I never told about this?" he would ask petulantly. "Why was it never brought to my attention? It's *very well written*."

Despite this excitement, Randolph's attention span being what it was, he lost the bet. He was distracted by the arrival of some Americans.

The war was winding down—Waugh's as well as England's—and soon Birkenhead was shipping out. He left with anxiety about his friends—"I felt sure that they must separate if yet another murder in the Balkans was to be averted." Soon, they did and it was. When Evelyn, ecstatic over his escape, arrived in Rome, he found a check for £50 waiting for him. Randolph was honoring his debt. He sent one to Birkenhead, too. It was the least that he could do.

—

AFTER THE WAR, relations between Evelyn Waugh and Randolph Churchill did not become more civilized. In fact, Randolph found civilian leisure more conducive to his trouble-making streak, going so far, in the early 1950s, as to share with Lord Norwich an insulting letter about him that Waugh had sent to Churchill. This caused a longer-lasting rift than had any squabble in Croatia.

But the fact is that they had great affection for each other. And when Randolph became ill, Waugh wrote in 1964 to his friend Lady Diana Cooper (Lord Norwich's wife), "I have become reconciled with Randolph. He looked so pathetically thin and feeble and when he tried to shout a whisper came. So 12 years enmity are expunged."

That war was over, too.

CHAPTER 6

The Home Fires Burning

—

ORWELL'S WAR WAS VERY DIFFERENT FROM WAUGH'S. NO fighting in foreign lands. Nothing to bring laughter at the retelling. But with all his failing strength he served his country, and Orwell's war was England's war. He was a foot soldier of the London blitz, and walked the burning streets with calm and resolution.

He was a member of the Home Guard. This was the lowest rung of the military, or even the paramilitary, ladder: voluntary, part-time, and unpaid. But, for its ragtag troopers, armed and in uniform, the Home Guard was the legion of honor in a capital under siege. The honor was won not so much through valor as by pluck, of which there is no better example than the shabby ex-Etonian whose lined and gaunt countenance showed no hint of concern, let alone fear.

The Home Guard was organized to fight invading Germans. When Winston Churchill spoke of battling the enemy on the beaches and in the streets, he was speaking of the Home Guard. It had more than a million members, those too young or too old or too infirm to join the regular forces. They relieved the army of some routine work, such as patrols and air-raid precautions. But the main idea of the Home Guard was to blanket the nation with an armed and (somewhat) trained resistance so that "no invader could travel more than a few miles through open country or more than a few hundred yards in the big towns without coming upon a knot of armed men. Morale can be relied on absolutely."

Orwell could experience nothing without considering its political ramifications. Cyril Connolly said, "Orwell was a political animal. . . . He could not blow his nose without moralizing on conditions in the handkerchief industry." So he soon imagined that the Home Guard would be a perfect nucleus for a mass revolt against the rich. Remembering the fierce resistance that armed Spanish workers had shown Franco, he happily noted, "Somewhere near a million British working men now have rifles in their bedrooms and don't in the least wish to give them up. The possibilities contained in that fact barely need pointing out." This is just as well, since none of those possibilities ever came to pass. At the end of the war, Churchill was replaced by the socialist Clement Attlee entirely by votes, not guns, which had been unhesitatingly returned when the threat of invasion had passed.

Orwell, regardless of the actual situation (including the fact that while guns were indeed widely distributed, ammunition was not), was euphoric about the arming of the proletariat. He wrote an article for Lord Beaverbrook's *Evening Standard* headlined "Don't Let Colonel Blimp Run the Home Guard." (British political cartoonist David Low had invented Colonel Blimp in the 1930s to embody a pompous, stupid, reactionary member of the upper class. Orwell loved the caricature.) In the *Evening Standard* article he wrote, "The Totalitarian states can do great things, but there is one thing they cannot do: they cannot give the factory-worker a rifle and tell him to take it home and keep it in his bedroom. THAT RIFLE HANGING ON THE WALL

OF THE WORKING CLASS FLAT OR LABORER'S COT-
TAGE IS THE SYMBOL OF DEMOCRACY. IT IS OUR
JOB TO SEE THAT IT STAYS THERE." It is not recorded
what Lord Beaverbrook thought on reading his daily.

More remarkable than Orwell joining the Home Guard during the blitz was that he was in London at all. He had moved
back from the country to be there, closing the unprofitable little store he and Eileen had been operating and trading the
safety and relative comfort of the country for the danger and
privation of wartime London. Conditions were difficult for
even the hardiest, and Orwell was virtually an invalid. Walking
up the stairs to his small apartment left him breathless. The
food rations were meager. The filth, the dust, the scarcity of little necessities like razor blades, the absence of any amenity, the
sleeplessness, the smells, the crowding, the sirens, the unre-
lieved unpleasantness of every aspect of life eventually became
the background of *1984*, where in many details they required
no exaggeration.

But Orwell chose to be in London. He wanted to be in the
thick of things, where the action was. And there was plenty of
action—the night sky ablaze and the streets full of rubble. Orwell was assigned to serve with the St. John's Woods volunteers, which, despite its bucolic name, was headquartered in
central London. Like all Home Guard outfits, it was an assort-
ment of all types of men except those fit for active duty. Because
of his experience with street fighting in Spain, Orwell was made
a sergeant and later fulfilled every writer's wish by being in
command of his publisher, Home Guard corporal Fred Warburg. (On the other hand, he found himself under the command of a former member of Oswald Mosley's Fascist
Blackshirts, who undoubtedly thought even less of that *Evening*

Standard piece than Beaverbrook had.) The group guarded the local telephone exchange and practiced lobbing chunks of concrete as if they were hand grenades. Orwell, to whom this struggle was not only against Hitler but the entire English class structure as well, threw himself into the effort. Eileen was beside herself: "I can put up with bombs on the mantelpiece, but I will not have a machine gun under the bed." Orwell's fervor exceeded his skills. He once loaded the wrong kind of bomb into a mortar, and when it was fired, the hapless volunteer directing it lost his front teeth and was unconscious for twenty-four hours.

Fortunately, the Home Guard was not Orwell's only form of wartime service. He also wrote. During the war years, under the most intolerable conditions, while serving part-time with the Home Guard, choosing to disregard a body weak and diseased, he created the best crafted and most enduring essays of his time. The world knows him now primarily for two short books, a fable and a warning, *Animal Farm* and *1984*. But the essays and reviews that preceded those books are as lasting a legacy. And there is nothing in the two novels—not a thought, not an insight—that doesn't reflect the lucid lines of the essays, which are, in fact, their foundation. Orwell's first rule of effective writing was to follow every general statement with a specific example from real life. *Animal Farm* and *1984* are the examples, as well as the distillate, of Orwell's nonfiction, his great body of immortal essays and reviews, one of the treasures of our culture.

He wrote most of them during only a few years. Orwell's nonfiction is encompassed in four famous volumes making up *The Collected Essays, Journalism and Letters of George Orwell.* Each volume is about five hundred pages long. Volume one contains work from 1920 to 1940; volume four, from 1945 until 1950. This means that over half his nonfiction output was crowded into a few war years, the thoughts of a lifetime expressed primarily near its end.

Why did he wait so long to write so much? The answer is tragic and maddening. He wrote relatively few articles before the war partly because no one would publish them. Magazines and journals rejected his nonfiction because he was known to be fiercely anticommunist. If he had been a conservative, then some (mostly small) publications might have been available. But he was a man of the Left—a socialist, on the side of the poor in a class war against the rich. There were plenty of journals on the left, but not for a writer who saw Stalin in the same way he saw Hitler.

But war, with all its hardships, provided a unique opportunity for Orwell. Other English writers went into the military, the government, or to America. There weren't many people left to write for all the journals. Orwell was ill and worn-down, and he devoted much time to the Home Guard, but he was in England, and his iron will ignored his maladies. He owned little but a typewriter, and now its output actually was being published.

And this made it possible for Orwell to find his audience. Soon, there were magazines that wanted his work—not because there was no one else but because they actually wanted *him*.

The first significant outlet for Orwell was *Horizon*, a literary monthly of great distinction that began publication in January 1940. Much of Orwell's best writing appeared there in the next few years. *Horizon* had a rich benefactor, Peter Watson, who avidly wanted the best writers, and a celebrated editor, Cyril

Connolly, the former classmate of both Blair and Waugh. Orwell and Connolly had renewed their friendship in the 1930s (on seeing Orwell after so many years Connolly "was appalled by the ravaged grooves that ran down from cheek to chin") and Connolly had written a favorable review of one of Orwell's books. (He had done him the far greater favor of introducing him to Eileen O'Shaughnessy at a London party years earlier.)

With Connolly's help, Orwell became a regular contributor to *Horizon*. And the BBC hired him to help with broadcasts designed to elicit support for Britain's war effort from listeners in India. This work was time-consuming and almost completely ineffective, but fairly well paid at £640 per year. At last he had an income that allowed him to write, which didn't stop Orwell and Eileen from giving away rations and money to those they thought needier than themselves. Even better than a modicum of economic independence was the chance to publish his work in a first-class and influential magazine. Connolly was politically of the Left, though not so far out on the spectrum as Orwell, whose dreams of the Home Guard storming the Ritz he found absurd. But as editor of *Horizon* he welcomed many points of view, an aberrant gesture in the London literary scene. (He also published work by Waugh, including, after the war, the entire text of Waugh's comic novel set in America, *The Loved One*, in a single edition of *Horizon*.)

But perhaps the best connection Connolly made for Orwell was recommending him to Clement Greenberg, editor of the *Partisan Review*, a small but increasingly influential magazine in New York intellectual circles. It had been an offspring of the leftist John Reed Club and quite pro-Soviet, but after infighting so fierce that some of the survivors didn't speak to one another for the next fifty years, it became what the losers of the struggle called "Trotskyite" and the winners described as reliably Left but passionately anticommunist. It was the perfect forum for Orwell, who wrote a "London Letter" for *Partisan Review* throughout the war. The pay was meager, but now he could reach an American audience, too.

For the first time Orwell could write knowing that his words would be published and read. He typed through sirens and air raids and after long hours of drilling with the Home Guard. He wrote about London during the blitz, and did so differently than anyone else. He wrote about political issues but also about everything else he found interesting, and what he put down on paper will be interesting forever. He wrote objectively and with astonishing clarity. His sad, kind eyes missed absolutely nothing. He described his foes with an evenhandedness that imploded their pomposity. Almost uniquely, he preached what he practiced. From his little garret under the searchlights, he marshaled the English language as freedom's finest force.

Here are some examples of the words he sent to war.

In an essay about Dickens, amazingly fresh in its insights ("The outstanding unmistakable mark of Dickens' writing is the *unnecessary detail*"), Orwell concludes by imaging the face that Dickens deserves: "It is the face of a man who is always fighting against something, but who fights in the open and is not frightened, the face of a man who is *generously angry*—in other words, of a nineteenth century liberal, a free intelligence, a type hated with equal hatred by all the smelly little orthodoxies which are now contending for our souls." This is a fair description of Orwell himself, and a sad prophecy as well, since the smelly little orthodoxies have now become even more malodorous.

Orwell argued that little first-rate prose had been written

during the prewar years, and he blamed this on the orthodoxies, too, because now "anyone sensitive enough to be troubled by the *zeitgeist* was also involved in politics" and "good novels are not written by orthodoxy-sniffers." The aversion to fashionable orthodoxy is why Orwell, consumed as he was with politics yet uncontaminated by political correctness, was able to write at least two great novels. And it also explains why Waugh, who cared nothing about politics, was able to write so many lasting novels.

Orwell pinned his hopes on the common people. "The thing that frightens one about the modern intelligentsia is their inability to see that human society must be based on common decency, whatever the political and economic forms might be. . . . My chief hope for the future is that the common people have never parted company with their moral code." This is not merely stating the obvious. It wasn't, and still isn't, obvious to the intellectual class of which he wrote. The failure to state values as well as policies has cost many good candidates electoral victory in our own time.

Unfettered by any orthodoxy, the mild-mannered Orwell was continually shocking. "I should like to put it on record that I have never been able to dislike Hitler," though he added, as an afterthought, that of course he would kill Hitler if he ever had the chance. Even the titles of his essays were provocative, as with "My Country Right or Left."

The power of his prose stemmed in part from his commitment to illustrating general principles with real-life examples:

Reading Mr. Malcolm Muggeridge's brilliant and depressing book, *The Thirties*, I thought of a rather cruel trick I once played on a wasp. He was sucking jam on my plate, and I cut him in half. He paid no attention, merely went on with his meal, while a tiny stream of jam trickled out of his severed esophagus. Only when he tried to fly away did he grasp the dreadful thing that had happened to him. It is the same with modern man. The thing that has been cut away is his soul, and there was a period—twenty years, perhaps—during which he did not notice it.

Like anyone who writes so much so fervently, Orwell, despite the simplicity and power of his prose, was sometimes spectacularly wrong. He liked Aldous Huxley's *Brave New World*, but thought "it had no relation to the actual future." Would that this were so. Sometimes his mistakes were obvious: "It is not certain that socialism is in all ways superior to capitalism, but it is certain that, unlike capitalism, it can solve the problems of production and consumption."

He thought that Hitler was winning the war because a planned economy would always outproduce a free-market economy. (He adjusted this opinion later in the war when American planes and ships were produced so quickly and in such astounding quantity that even Churchill found it hard to believe the numbers.) Of course, war production in America *was* centralized for the duration, but it relied heavily on factories that originally had been developed for consumer production, such as Ford plants. American ration books looked like banquet menus to the British, and the production of consumer goods after the war went through the roof. So Orwell's blunt declaration in 1941 that "laissez-faire capitalism is dead" is a howler. He added, "It is interesting to notice that Mr. [Joseph] Kennedy, USA Ambassador in London, remarked on his return to New

York in October 1940 that as a result of the war 'democracy is finished'. By 'democracy', of course, he meant private capital-ism." Actually, by "democracy," Kennedy meant democracy, and he was as wrong as Orwell. Which could be pretty wrong.

In 1942, Orwell informed his American readers that Churchill would be out of office in a few months. He didn't think that India could be a sovereign state. He asked despair-ingly, as if the answer were obvious, "What instance is there of a modern industrialized state collapsing, unless conquered from the outside by military force?" The eventual fall of the Soviet empire as it actually occurred was then inconceivable to him.

But these errors also demonstrated Orwell's greatest virtue: When he found out he had made a mistake or a prediction had been wrong, he admitted it, publicly, in print. He made a point of it. This tells us more about George Orwell than any other fact. He believed passionately in objective reality. If something that was proved false remained in print then that error re-mained a brick in the wall of lies he saw going up in every land. The worst aspect of the future nightmare he described in *1984* was that "truth" was subjective; the facts could be changed to fit the whim of the rulers, and frequently were. When obvious facts disproved the predictions of Stalin or Hitler, those dicta-tors simply changed their earlier statements in the history books and newspapers of the countries under their control. Or-well refused to play that game, and if admitting error made him seem less prescient, or wise, that was not as important as setting the record straight.

So in a "London Letter" to *Partisan Review* in 1945, he took full blame for saying "laissez-faire capitalism is dead," since by the war's end it was clear, he admitted, that "the United States is indeed the most powerful country in the world, and the most capitalistic." He also confessed in print that his prediction about how long Churchill would stay in office had been spectacularly mistaken.

He was honest when he was wrong, but when he was right, as he most often was, he was sublime. On why totalitarianism is so much worse than even imperfect democracy: "It is the difference between land power and sea power, between cruelty and inefficiency, between lying and self-deception, between the SS man and the rent-collector." These were easy choices for Orwell, and for almost everyone else in the world, except for most of the opinion leaders of his time.

His words are easy to read and hard to forget. "It is commonly said that every human being has in him the material for one good book, which is true in the same sense as it is true that every block of stone contains a statue." "England is a family with the wrong members in control." Rich young people are switching their allegiance from Stalin to Gandhi so that "in the name of 'spirituality' you can keep your money." "A humanitarian is always a hypocrite." "We live in an age in which the average human being in the highly civilized countries is aesthetically inferior to the lowest savage." "No one is patriotic about taxes." "Saints should always be judged guilty until they are proved innocent."

He wrote about everything: about writers, about the war, about good bad books and overrated classics. He wrote a long essay on Jonathan Swift in which Swift comes out seeming just like Waugh; he wrote scathingly about Salvador Dali as a symbol of all that was wrong with the modern world; he wrote a lovely piece on the return of the common toad to England in the spring, and somehow managed even with that subject to make a political point; he wrote about boys' magazines and why Tolstoy was wrong about Shakespeare; he wrote about anti-Semitism in Britain when everyone else was writing about it in Germany; he wrote grimly about the future and lovingly about the past; he wrote about the significance of cuffs on trousers. Everything he wrote was fresh and readable and completely free from what was then in fashion.

Although the gentlest of men, Orwell could not write an essay without making some people angry. He infuriated the Labour Party by noting calmly that the standard of living enjoyed by union members in Britain depended on the sweat of Indian coolies. British pacifists were angered almost to combat when he wrote that their nonviolence was made possible by the protection of the British navy. He shocked everyone by asking why nineteen-year-old soldiers should be thought more expendable than old people. He even defended snobbishness, because it "is a check upon behavior whose value from a social point of view has been underrated." (Not by Waugh.) Perhaps most shocking of all, he published his phone number (CAN 3751) in a *Partisan Review* column so that any American readers who got to England in uniform could call him up and chat. Several of them did so, thus intruding on a busy—and terminally ill—writer's privacy and time.

It is no wonder that American soldiers who read Orwell in the 1940s wanted to meet him. There was no other voice like his. Once people started reading him they wanted to read more. And they were able to do so, as other papers and journals started publishing his pieces. After he left the BBC, he started a regular column, "As I Please," for the London *Observer*.

Orwell was beginning to be known as a major writer. The small outlets through which his words flowed became tributaries to an ever-widening public. He never kept a diary in the way that Waugh did, though he had started a war diary in collaboration with Inez Holden, a fellow writer and close friend. The project was dropped, but she went on to publish her own. It contains a perfect description of Orwell's growing stature as early as September 1941:

> It's strange the way a writer's fame begins slowly creeping up to him and then racing so that after a while he seems to be a poor relation of his own fame. People of taste and sensitiveness, writers, political workers and actors (who are now showing signs of being extremely left wing), socialist doctors, factory workers and technical instructors in touch with their labor organizations are all well aware of Orwell.
>
> Yesterday at the P.E.N. world congress lunch I sat at a table with [Arthur] Koestler, Cyril Connolly, Stevie Smith, Guy Chapman, Koestler's girl friend Miss Hardy . . . Rene Avord, of *la France Libre,* who has some other name, and a German refugee writer. Koestler was betting that Orwell would be the greatest best seller in five years time and our bet was five bottles of burgundy.

Lucky Koestler. One hopes he named a good vintage, because seldom has a wager been so spectacularly won, although less quickly than it should have been. It was only about two years until *Animal Farm* was written, but the book wasn't published until 1945 for reasons difficult to believe today.

Orwell's usual publisher was Victor Gollancz. They had been associated for many years, ever since Gollancz had published *Down and Out in Paris and London*. It was on that occasion that Blair, not wanting to use his real name, had made out a list of alternatives, and Gollancz, reviewing the possible pseudonyms, had voted for "George Orwell." This beat out "Kenneth Miles" and—honestly—"H. Lewis Allways." And it was Gollancz who had commissioned Orwell to go to the north to report on conditions of the unemployed there, resulting in *The Road to Wigan Pier*.

But however helpful Gollancz had been in the past, Orwell thought he would never agree to publish *Animal Farm* because he was head of the communist-dominated Left Book Club. *Animal Farm* is obviously based on the Russian Revolution and what it produced. The Communist Party members are the pigs; their leader Napoleon is Stalin; Snowball is Leon Trotsky; and so on. Since the theme is the betrayal of the animals' revolution by power-hungry pigs who become just like the cruel humans who preceded them, the book would be seen at once as an attack on Stalin and his regime. It is, in fact, an attack on all totalitarians, but since the farm-as-Russia parable is the example employed, then naturally the Soviets would be the most offended.

This is not something that Gollancz would want to do. Still, as Orwell's publisher, he had the right of first refusal, which means he had to reject the manuscript before it could be sent to any other publisher. So Orwell sent a note to Gollancz saying he had a book to submit but warning that the manuscript was "completely unacceptable politically from your point of view (it is anti-Stalin)."

Gollancz sent back a note of injured honor. How could anyone think he would be afraid to offend Stalin? The Soviets themselves, he claimed, considered him an anti-Stalinist. He seemed terribly hurt by this slur on his objectivity. He asked to be sent the manuscript.

Orwell sent it. Gollancz replied with lightning speed.

APRIL 4, 1944

My dear Blair,

You are right and I was wrong. I am so sorry. I have returned the manuscript to Moore [Orwell's agent].

Yours sincerely,
Dictated by Mr. Gollancz
but signed in his absence.

The alacrity and brevity of his response—he was dropping this hot potato lest anyone think he had actually ordered it— amused Orwell. He had never *wanted* Gollancz to publish his book. He knew how good it was and was looking for a major publisher. One of the best publishers in England was Jonathan Cape, so Orwell sent it to him. Cape's chief reader favored publication, as did the assistant reader. Cape wanted to publish it, and began discussing contract terms with Orwell's agent.

And then he did something that is still hard to believe. Since the manuscript raised "a matter of policy," he thought he'd better talk it over with a friend of his, a senior official in the Ministry of Information. The high-placed government official, unnamed for years thereafter, sent a strong letter back to Cape urging him not to publish a book that would damage Britain's relations with Russia.

Cape claimed to be anguished, but he acted with haste. He fired off a pathetic letter to Orwell's agent.

I mentioned the reaction that I had from an important official in the Ministry of Information with regard to ANIMAL FARM. I must confess that the expression of opinion has given me seriously to think. My reading of the manuscript gave me considerable personal enjoyment . . . but I can see now that it might be regarded as something which it was highly ill-advised to publish at the present time. . . . Another thing: it would be less offensive if the predominant caste in the fable were not pigs. I think the choice of pigs as the ruling caste will no doubt give offence to many people, and particularly to anyone who is a bit touchy, as undoubtedly the Russians are. . . . I think it is best to send back to you the typescript of ANIMAL FARM and let the matter lie on the table as far as we are concerned. . . .

> Yours Sincerely,
> Jonathan Cape

The phrase "let the matter lie on the table" can be loosely translated as "we wouldn't touch this baby with a ten-foot pole." The agent sent a copy of Cape's letter to Orwell, whose immediate reaction is still visible on the margin of the letter, on which he has scribbled "balls." The translation of *this* would be that the Russians would surely object to this book even if he changed his pigs to rabbits.

For those who think the story cannot possibly become worse, just wait. The high official at the Ministry of Information was, in fact, one Peter Smollett. Though neither Cape nor Orwell knew this at the time—perhaps no Englishman did— Mr. Smollett was a Soviet agent.

This is a sordid tale. The fact that Smollett was working for the Soviets is really no worse than that a publisher in a democracy felt he must clandestinely share a manuscript with the government before he would publish it.

Orwell's efforts to publish his book did not get any easier. He was upset, but he knew that Cape wasn't the only major publisher in town. There was also Faber & Faber, one of whose active partners was T. S. Eliot. Orwell was well acquainted with Eliot. He sent him the manuscript.

T. S. Eliot, it can safely be said, was not a Soviet agent. Eliot was arguably the greatest living poet, and would win the Nobel Prize for Literature in 1948. He was a highly devout member of the Church of England and a political conservative who detested communism.

Within a few days Orwell received a letter back from Eliot, and the speed of the reply must have been heartening.

But then he opened the envelope. The letter started out well enough. Eliot compared Orwell to Swift. He found *Animal Farm* "a distinguished piece of writing."

But there were other considerations. "We have no conviction," wrote Eliot, "that this is the right point of view from which to criticize the political situation at the present time." The present time was July 1944, about a month after the Normandy invasion. The second front had been established. The first front was being fought by the Russians, second only to America as England's strongest ally. The desire to avoid offending an ally at the height of a war is understandable. But one of the things that England was fighting for was freedom of speech. The refusal to publish in England a fable critical of Stalin was contemptible. And pointless as well: When the book did come out in England, it made no difference in Britain's relations with Russia.

There is a phrase: adding insult to injury. A very fine example would be Eliot's next epistolary point. "After all," the poet wrote, "your pigs are far more intelligent than the other animals, and therefore the best qualified to run the farm." We don't know Orwell's immediate response, but he may by this time have been musing that he ought to have made his villains squirrels.

Quite understandably, Orwell became desperate. He considered publishing the book himself.

And then he found a publisher, though not one he would have initially sought. Secker & Warburg had published Orwell's *Homage to Catalonia,* and Fred Warburg was one of Orwell's closest friends (despite having served under his command in the Home Guard). But it was a relatively small house and had a reputation for being "Trotskyite." Orwell had wanted a major and politically neutral publisher for a book that he knew could reach a wide audience. But he had tried the majors and struck out. (He had even made an effort to find an American publisher, but Dial Press turned it down with the statement that it was impossible to sell animal stories in the U.S.A. Nonpolitical publishers had blinders of their own.)

So Orwell signed with Warburg and handed over the now dog-eared manuscript of *Animal Farm.* This gave Secker & Warburg the right to publish Orwell's next book, too, and that was *1984.* A better day's work was probably never done in all the annals of publishing. Because of paper shortages, *Animal Farm* did not come out until August 1945. By the time of Warburg's death, in 1981, it had sold nine million copies, and *1984,* eleven million. That number is far greater now, and both books still sell briskly. They are part of our culture. They have altered our vocabulary, and they have focused our minds. They have defended our freedom.

The enormous difficulties Orwell faced in his efforts to publish *Animal Farm* are important because the same difficulties exist today. Not with regard to offending communists, of course. Not many years after *Animal Farm* came out the author of a pro-Stalin book in the United States would have had an experience comparable to Orwell's. It is wrong to constrain political thought, even bad political thought. And if the targets of political correctness have changed over the years, its power over what gets printed, heard, or seen has not. This may, in fact, be more a problem now than then.

England has no written constitution, and therefore no First Amendment. But even if there had been a British Bill of Rights it would have offered no protection to Orwell in this matter. The First Amendment does not require a publisher to print anything the publisher doesn't want to—because publishers have rights, too. If a law were passed prohibiting the expression of certain views, it would be held unconstitutional. But political correctness is not a law. That's why it's so dangerous. Its victims have no constitutional protections. And even today it prevents the expression of uncomfortable truths more effectively than any statute ever could.

If Orwell were with us today, he would probably welcome the Internet blogs as an alternative to the mainstream political correctness that almost kept him from print. (He would have faulted the blogs on other grounds.) Of course, Orwell *is* with us today, but that was a very close call.

CHAPTER 7

Yes, We Have No Bananas

—

ISTORY IS FILLED WITH GREAT MEN WHO HAD NO time for their own children. How would Orwell and Waugh be judged in this regard? The answer matters, since both insisted that good works begin at home.

Evelyn Waugh as a father has become something of a legend, and a shocking one at that, but as with so many legends, this one is largely false.

Laura Herbert Waugh gave birth to seven children. All but one survived. (Mary was born in 1940 and baptized, but lived only a day. The last of the Waugh children was given the name Septimus, to note and honor the fact that there were not merely six children, but seven human lives whom God had granted the Waughs.)

The first child, Teresa, was born in 1938, less than a year after Evelyn and Laura were married. Her full name is Maria Teresa. She was born just as Hitler annexed Austria and the newborn's father wanted to make a statement that Austria was not Hitler's; it was a Catholic country as personified by Maria Theresa, archduchess of Austria and wife of the Holy Roman emperor Francis I.

The longed-for son arrived in 1939, and was named Auberon. The choice of name is instructive. It was very much a

Herbert name, and has nothing whatsoever to do with Shakespeare's Oberon. It supposedly was invented by Laura's great-grandfather Henry, the third Earl of Carnarvon, on naming his son, who then gave the name to *his* son. Auberon is pronounced "Orbr'n" by the Herberts, who apparently had exclusive possession of the name. Auberon Waugh's son Alexander has written, "to the best of my knowledge there have only ever been eight Auberons and all descend from Henry Carnarvon."

Of course, there would have been no Waugh children at all if Laura Herbert had listened to the advice of her brother Auberon on the way to the wedding chapel and left Evelyn waiting at the altar. The groom never got over his rage that Auberon had deemed him unsuitable. As target of both scorn and vengeance, Auberon Herbert became the newest Cruttwell.

And yet Evelyn Waugh named his firstborn son Auberon, when he loathed the only other Auberon he knew, because it was a Herbert name. Only Herberts had it. If Evelyn Waugh was going to have Herbert children, then by God they would have Herbert names. And now they were Waugh names, too. Indeed, the *Oxford Dictionary of Names* says that Auberon means "noble bear," and gives, as if in proof, this example: "as in Auberon Herbert and Auberon Waugh." Apparently the provenance of the name offset for Evelyn Waugh any personal association it had, however galling.

(Not to worry. The grievance against Auberon Herbert was not forgotten. The wound stayed open even unto the generations. The insatiability of Waugh retribution has proved heritable—in his exceptionally fine and funny book about Waugh pères pairs, *Fathers and Sons,* Evelyn's grandson Alexander, son and father of Auberon, strongly suggests that his great-uncle Auberon was not in fact a Herbert at all, but the illegitimate son of the author Hilaire Belloc. So who was this bastard to say who should or should not marry into the Herbert family? Somewhere up there the ghost of Evelyn is smiling at his grandson's act of filial fealty.)

Auberon was followed by the sadly short-lived Mary. Then, in 1942, Margaret arrived—she would be unquestionably her father's favorite. Harriet was born in 1944 and James in 1946.

With the exception of Septimus, born in 1950, all these children arrived about as swiftly as nature allows, one right after another, and all the rest save Teresa were born when Britain was at war. These were years in which their father was in uniform and often far from home. It seemed as if every furlough was followed nine months later by a birth. Waugh also managed to write two books during the same crowded time, the sublime and hilarious *Put Out More Flags* and his magnum opus, *Brideshead Revisited*. It was in every way the most productive period of his life.

After the war he returned to Piers Court. It is unfair to judge him as a father until that point, because like most British fathers of young children then, he was separated from his family by military service.

It is the subsequent years that have caused many to question just how good a father he was. He had been fighting in part to preserve the concept of private life, and now he had a chance to live it in a house filled with his children.

How well did he live this part of private life, his life as a father? So many people have already raised this question, and they have done so for three reasons. Three episodes, actually, each spectacular enough to have become part of the Waugh legend, and none, it must be conceded, very flattering to him.

First, there is the matter of the bananas.

And here some prefatory history may be helpful.

During the Second World War, the Germans blockaded the British Isles with a ring of submarines, making it difficult for England to import supplies. Military equipment, oil, and other necessities for defense had the highest priority. Food did not.

England, of course, produces its own food. Bread and butter and fish and, to some extent, meat, were available, though severely rationed.

But fruit was a different matter. So for more than six years no tropical fruit was seen in England, and schoolchildren knew what it looked like from pictures in their books, but had no idea how these strange-looking things tasted.

People covet what they cannot have. When Alexander Korda, the film producer, arrived in Hollywood from wartime Britain, he knew what the perfect gift would be and arranged to have oranges sent to Prime Minister Churchill. This took some doing. They had to be sent by air to New York, and then to London in the very precious cargo space of a British bomber, and then rushed to Churchill. The prime minister was thrilled and grateful to have such treasures, and Korda was soon knighted, the first member of the movie industry to be so honored.

When the war was over, the new Labour government, anxious to prove the years of austerity were over (they were not), distributed bananas to the children of Britain. The great banana distribution was meant to represent bounty renewed. It was all done with coupons—one coupon, one banana, for each child.

By this time the Waughs had three children eligible to receive bananas. Laura went into town and used her coupons. She brought the bananas home. Evelyn then summoned the three children to the dining room. The bananas were brought in and placed on the table. The children gaped, and leaned forward.

What happened next was astounding. "All three [bananas] were put on my father's plate, and before the anguished eyes of his children, he poured on cream, which was almost unprocurable, and sugar, which was heavily rationed, and ate all three. . . . From that moment I never treated anything he had to say on faith or morals very seriously."

These were the words of Auberon Waugh, Evelyn's son, in his autobiography written nearly half a century after watching the ravishment not only of his food but apparently his faith.

The story's publication caused quite a stir. Evelyn Waugh was long gone by then, but still in the spotlight, and commentators concluded almost unanimously that the banana episode exemplified his family life.

In *Fathers and Sons*, Auberon's son Alexander raises the possibility that the banana story may have been invented. However, Auberon's elder sister, Teresa Waugh D'Arms, a keeper of her father's flame but scrupulously fair, concedes that she remembers the gluttonous deed. After all, one of those bananas was supposed to be hers.

This does not make her father a Beast. He was, however, like his own father, a consummate and irrepressible actor. The odds are good that the whole banana episode was just an act. It's the sort of thing that Evelyn Waugh did. Acting kept people off guard; it kept people *away*.

And it added to his legend. He *liked* being thought a Beast.

Outrageous as it was, the banana incident is not devoid of a certain element of humor. But the second episode that marred Waugh's reputation as a father, though even more startling than the first, has nothing humorous about it at all. It is simply sad.

At eighteen, Auberon Waugh was a young officer doing his military service in Cyprus. At that time, 1958, the island was still a Crown colony and in a state of emergency due to fierce hostilities between its Turk and Greek inhabitants. Out on patrol one hot day in June, Bron (as he was called) noticed a problem with the elevation of the machine gun on his armored car. He stopped and walked over to the front of the car. Facing the machine gun, he tried to shake it back into place. The gun began to fire— directly into the chest of Auberon Waugh. He leapt away, but six bullets had already struck him, four through the chest and shoulder, one through the arm, and one through the left hand.

Bron was sure he was dying, a view shared by those who saw his bleeding body stretched out on the ground. He was rushed to a hospital, where his lung, spleen, and some ribs were removed. The last rites were administered. He was in critical condition, his chances of survival very much in doubt.

The fame of his father turned the second lieutenant's accident into a headline story in the London press.

MRS WAUGH FLIES TO BEDSIDE OF WOUNDED SON

Mrs Evelyn Waugh, wife of the novelist, will fly to Cyprus today to visit her 18-year old son, accidentally shot. . . . His mother said: "My flight has been arranged by the Red Cross and I hope to leave London airport early tomorrow. My husband will remain at home."

"My husband will remain at home." With his son hovering between life and death for weeks in a sweltering Cypriot hospital, why did Waugh not join his wife in her vigil at Bron's bedside? How could he remain in England?

Apparently it was because he was writing a book—the biography of the recently deceased Monsignor Ronald Knox, whom Waugh had greatly admired as priest, writer, and friend. As always when writing, Waugh was relentlessly disciplined in adherence to his work.

One can make other excuses for his refusal to leave home: Laura was perfectly capable of overseeing Bron's care, and Waugh's health was bad—he had had a major breakdown a few years earlier, intensified by excessive medication. He had not only recovered but written a remarkably fine and funny book about his temporary insanity, *The Ordeal of Gilbert Pinfold*. Nonetheless, he may well have feared a relapse.

But when all is said and done, the truth is that he stayed put largely because of his writing. For Waugh, work always took precedence, even over his family. When he was courting Laura Herbert, he wrote her a remarkable letter, the entire point of which was to sell himself as good husband material. It's a very clever letter, in which a sorcerer turns his brass into gold. And then, at the end, just as his words seem sure to close the deal, he gives for the sake of fairness a warning: "My only tie of any kind is my work. That means that for several months each year we shall have to separate or you would have to share some very lonely place with me." He's undercutting his case, but it's such an important point to him that honor requires he mention it as a condition of marriage. Of course, Bron, unlike his mother, never had the chance to sign off on this point.

Bron eventually recovered. He lost a finger, as well as various organs and bones, and probably some years of his life, but he recovered. He recuperated in a London hospital for many months, and his father was an attentive visitor. The book had been finished by then.

The third rap on Waugh the father should not be taken seriously, even though, or perhaps because, it comes from the pen of Waugh himself. It comes from his diary, to which he confided throughout his life. That diary was a ticking time bomb. When, in 1978, more than a decade after his death, Laura shared it with the world, it detonated quite spectacularly, with considerable collateral damage to former schoolmates and famous friends. But the principal victim of the explosion was without question the author. Waugh's comments on his children caused sharp intakes of breath and the sad shaking of heads.

There it all was, and in his own hand. And many times. It was almost a theme: He wrote that he was alternately bored or repulsed by his offspring.

August 24, 1946: "A tedious three days among my children."

December 23, 1946: "The presence of my children affects me with deep weariness and depression. I do not see them until luncheon, as I have my breakfast alone in the library, and they are in fact well trained to avoid my part of the house; but I am aware of them from the moment I wake. Luncheon is very painful. Teresa has a mincing habit of speech and a pert, humourless style of wit; Bron is clumsy and disheveled, sly, without intellectual, aesthetic or spiritual interest; Margaret is pretty and below the age of reason. In the nursery whooping cough rages I believe."

April 19, 1947: "My children afford me no pleasure."

And so on. People were aghast or angry at the self-painted portrait of the callous parent.

Yet very likely, like those damned bananas, the diary entries were part of an act. To be sure, there was some truth in them. No doubt the easily bored and fastidious man of letters was indeed put out by the clamor and incessancy of six spirited young children. Even the most saintly parents, to whose company Evelyn Waugh could scarcely aspire, will on occasion lose control. When that happens, however, they usually try to keep it to themselves. But Waugh wrote these shocking comments not only in his diary, but in letters to his closest friends—in many cases very prominent friends. For example, on January 5, 1946, he wrote to Nancy Mitford, "My two eldest children are here and a great bore. . . . The boy lives for pleasure and is thought a great wit by his contemporaries. I have tried him drunk and I have tried him sober." Waugh must have known that even if he didn't publish his letters to Mitford, she would. And did. He might as well have written a letter about his children to *The Times*.

Which is one of the reasons we can doubt that Waugh meant these words of disparagement. He was performing a role all his life, and words uttered onstage are never the same as the actor's real thoughts. Waugh, a great natural actor, the son and grandson of great natural actors, knew his limitations in the roles he might assay. Hamlet was too indecisive for his temperament; Lear would suit him better; Falstaff was perfect. Waugh could do outrageous and comic better than any mere professional on the stage. It was all in the service of validating his new class identity. When he realized he couldn't do a completely convincing haughty duke he settled for the fierce and puffy country squire, one of the meatier roles in the upper-class repertoire. He built up his part through wardrobe, sets, and audacity. And to more convincingly portray the testy patroon he dragged his children into the act, by dropping little clues to parental enmity where he knew they would be found.

Of course, it wasn't *all* an act. As has been noted, he was exceptionally sensitive to slights. When his children, being children, did not show their full appreciation of his parental efforts, he retaliated. (Never physically.) If he spent the day taking Bron to the zoo and buying him treats and then the sated son seemed less than grateful, Waugh took it personally. In the same diary entry, December 23, 1946, in which he claims his children cause him "deep weariness and depression," scarcely an example of yuletide joy, he notes, "I used to take some pleasure in inventing legends for them about Basil Bennett, Dr. Bedlam and the Sebag-Montifores. But now they think it ingenuous to squeal: 'It isn't true!' " It seems that the real reason for his expressed depression is that his children were no longer beguiled by his fantastic stories, willfully libelous fictions they once had found diverting. As an eternal child, he was furious when his own offspring deserted him for adolescence.

His diary was both confessional and billboard. He confided to it the irritations to which all parents are prone, and portrayed himself as a curmudgeon in order to shock and impress the wide audience for which his supposedly private musings were actually intended.

The truth, despite the pains he took to distort it, is that Evelyn Waugh was a loving father. His children, even after the loss of their bananas, loved him back. When Bron was in the London hospital recovering from his accident, he was much cheered by his father's frequent visits. One day, however, complications set in and the patient once again believed he was near death. He scrawled a letter and wrote on the back of its sealed envelope, "For my father E. Waugh in the event of my predeceasing him, Auberon Waugh." He sent the letter to his bank with instructions to deliver it after his death. Bron recovered, and so the letter was never delivered. After Evelyn's death, the bank returned the letter to Bron, who put it at the bottom of an old chest. It was found there many years later by Bron's son Alexander, who read and shared its contents:

> Dear Papa,
>   Just a line to tell you what for some reason I was never able to show you in my lifetime, that I admire, revere and love you more than any other man in the world. . . .
>
>   Love, Bron.

That he was loved does not prove he was loving, but it does make the monster image harder to accept. Waugh sent his children to boarding schools when they were quite young, but so did virtually every other upper-class family at the time. At least he wrote to them and kept a sharp eye on how they were doing, which was more than some. When the very young Winston Churchill was at boarding school he read by chance in the local newspaper that his father, Lord Randolph Churchill, had given a speech near the school on the previous day. It was the first he knew of his father's recent proximity; Lord Randolph did not take the time to visit him, even for a moment. People all too often do unto others what was done to them, and Winston Churchill does not seem to have been a more attentive father than Lord Randolph had been to him. Perhaps that was why Winston's son, Randolph, led such a sad and besotted life. Waugh disliked Winston Churchill because he believed him to have been "a rotten father" to his son. That Waugh detested someone for being an unloving father suggests he *wanted* to be a better one, not through duty but because he loved his children.

He did not spend much time with his children and was far too honest to pretend that what association they did have was "quality time," a contemporary phrase he would have found appalling. He saw his children primarily at luncheon, a meal served in the dining room, where everyone was expected to converse. In the evening, Evelyn and Laura Waugh dined alone, he in black tie and she in a long dress. By the standards of the upper class the children were lucky even to have been included in the luncheon. And their father's absence in the morning was due to his efforts to support his family by writing. In the afternoon he spent considerable time with his wife, which was not a bad thing for the children to observe, and again, much less typical of the upper class.

As a father, Evelyn Waugh was wildly eccentric, sometimes hurtful, consistently insistent on the discipline of faith, and inherently devoted to his children, which they knew. By the standards of most great men, he wasn't a bad father at all.

GEORGE ORWELL WANTED very much to be a father, particularly to a son. But after eight years of marriage he and Eileen remained childless. Orwell concluded, without any medical opinion to support this, that he was infertile, and so they decided to adopt a baby.

Eileen was not so sure. She was tired and depressed, and much sicker than she let her husband know. Her beloved brother, Dr. Laurence O'Shaughnessy, the focus of her life until her marriage, had been killed on the beach at Dunkirk while trying to assist the wounded. Eileen never fully recovered from this loss. She was devoted to her husband, as once she had been to her brother. The brother seems to have been more grateful for her efforts. Orwell, like Waugh, was devoted primarily to his work. But while Waugh would retreat to a country hotel or to his sacrosanct study in order to write, Orwell could afford no such isolation and so just typed away incessantly in their tiny flat. He loved his wife, on his own terms, but was oblivious to her when he was working and less than faithful when he was not. Eileen had no illusions on either score, but in every sense she cared for her husband. Though she was exhausted by ill health and a full-time job at the Ministry of Food, she agreed to go ahead with the adoption. They heard of a young woman who had just given birth to a baby boy, the son of a Canadian soldier who had been stationed in England. She wanted to give the infant up for adoption. In June 1944, Eileen brought the baby home. They named him Richard Horatio Blair, after one of Orwell's ancestors, a captain in the Royal Navy during the nineteenth century.

Any doubts that Eileen may have had about adoption were displaced by joy as soon as Richard arrived. She quit her job to be with him. Orwell was ecstatic, too. The stern and unyielding prophet became a warm and affectionate father.

And a very traditional one in several regards. While he had chosen a life of grim austerity for himself, he immediately declared that Richard should have a first-class perambulator with gold trim. What's more, he put down the infant's name for boarding school! He even considered Eton, but, no doubt provoked by the memory of St. Cyprian's, registered Richard as a day student at Westminster, one of the most elite schools in the land (though one that had, unlike Eton, at least discontinued the requirement that its boys wear top hats).

These were Orwell's happiest years since early childhood. The war was ending, the danger of bombing had passed, and *Animal Farm* was about to be published, despite all the efforts to suppress it. He and Eileen were enthralled with the baby and had never been so close.

In February 1945 came more good news. Orwell, despite his health, had been approved as a war correspondent. He went to Europe, first to newly liberated Paris and then to those parts of Germany already under Allied control. If he could not be a soldier in battle, as Waugh had been, he could at least now feel that he was part of the great struggle on the continent.

One thing bothered him. He had never gotten over his hatred of the communists, who had come close to murdering him in Spain. Now he was about to come out with a book that satirized the Soviet regime. The Russians knew of it and were furious, so Orwell thought it possible that another attempt might be made to kill him. He had heard that the French communists were shooting their enemies—not all of them Germans—and felt the need to defend himself. At the time, it was very difficult for a civilian in Europe to buy a gun, but Orwell had an idea. He heard that Ernest Hemingway, whom he had never met, was also in Paris as a war correspondent; Orwell assumed, as a reader of Hemingway, that *he* was someone who very likely would have a gun. So, improbably enough, Orwell went over to the Ritz and found Hemingway's room. He introduced himself and explained the situation. Hemingway's private view was that Orwell's fears were ridiculous, but he had greatly admired *Homage to Catalonia* and so in homage to Orwell lent him his gun, a Colt .32. Thus armed, Orwell resumed his work as a war correspondent, presumably less worried about assassination.

But he missed his family. Now, for the first time, he felt that he truly *had* a family. "I hear that [Richard] has 5 teeth and is beginning to move about a lot," he wrote to a friend. Orwell went to Germany and sent back dispatches on the bombing of Cologne. But his health was bad. He hemorrhaged, and, returning to Paris, was hospitalized.

He did not know it, but back home Eileen, too, was in terrible health—worse even than his own. She had been aware for some time that something was very wrong. She suspected it was cancer but had not told her husband, because she knew how much he wanted to travel to Germany to cover the war. She didn't even see a doctor until after the paperwork on Richard's adoption was completed, fearing that her condition might preclude the baby being given over to her care.

When she finally saw a doctor, her fears were confirmed. She had tumors on her uterus and was suffering from internal bleeding, requiring a hysterectomy. She wrote to her husband that surgery was imminent. She was admitted to a hospital in Newcastle, where her sister-in-law lived. She was wheeled into the operating room. The anesthetic was administered. A few minutes later she was dead.

The operation had not even begun. She died of heart failure. The coroner's inquest concluded that the anesthetic had been properly administered and the doctors were not to blame. Eileen O'Shaughnessy Blair was thirty-nine years old.

There was still hardly any phone service between England and France. Orwell learned of his wife's death by telegram and then took the first flight of his life, on a military plane to London.

Love had made the stoic vulnerable—love for Eileen, late-realized and laden with guilt, and love for Richard, which was strong enough to withstand any suffering.

Always honest, he acknowledged his failings as a husband. "I was sometimes unfaithful to Eileen," he wrote to a friend, but in the same paragraph qualified: "What matters is being faithful in an emotional and intellectual sense. . . . It was a real marriage in the sense that we had been through awful struggles together and she understood all about my work." The last phrase shows his highest priority, even when grieving for his wife.

But though he may not have realized it then, or perhaps ever, from that point on he no longer lived only for his work. He also lived for Richard.

Richard was eleven months old when Eileen died in 1945. Many friends suggested that Orwell give him up to another family. This was understandable: Orwell was terribly ill and frail. He seemed incapable of caring for himself, let alone an infant. The idea of a father as single parent seemed far less possible at that time than today.

But Orwell would not hear of losing Richard. Richard was his *son*. He loved him deeply and simply. Family life, which was to Waugh as ritualized as his religion, was to Orwell the unaffected pleasure of being with his son.

He found a dream nanny, the twenty-seven-year-old Susan Watson, herself the mother of a seven-year-old. Susan was in the process of divorcing her husband, a Cambridge don. She was bright and kind and kept house and cooked for father and son—the son being easier to clean up after than the chain-smoking father.

She was well paid. For the first time in his life, Orwell had some money to spend. *Animal Farm* was successful from the start. But no one realized yet how much more successful it would be, throughout the world and to this day, or that the work still to be written by this sick and dying man would not only outshine his first success but reach iconic status and cause the very word "Orwellian" to permanently enter the language.

Upon receiving his first royalties, far more money than he'd ever had before, Orwell made what under the circumstances seemed a very strange decision. He decided to move to Scotland. Not just anywhere in Scotland. In fact, not really *in* Scotland at all. He bought a home on the island of Jura, in the Hebrides, sixteen miles off Scotland's west coast. This was where he and Richard were going to live.

Jura has been called "one of the most unappealing and inaccessible places in the British Isles." This description is somewhat flattering. It took forty-eight hours to journey from London to Orwell's home on Jura, and the last seven miles could be traversed only on foot. It seems always to have been raining there, and not the soft drizzle of England that makes roses perfect and cheeks rosy, but rather an unceasing downpour. Jura was so grim and desolate that it has been called "a cross between Wuthering Heights and Cold Comfort Farm."

So why on earth did Orwell move to Jura? It was a decision that puzzled his friends then and his fans now. This was the man so ill that he couldn't cover the Allied advance without collapsing. He had hemorrhaged in the London flat he shared with Richard, and without Susan Watson's swift ministrations might not have recovered. Why would a man with tuberculosis go to a damp and frigid island that even the Scots seem to have avoided?

Perhaps he was remembering his torments at St. Cyprian's. His principles, his politics, his astonishing devotion to destroying the class system, all stemmed from St. Cyprian's, where the most sensitive soul in the world had felt a boot upon his face.

And in the essay "Such, Such Were the Joys," still to be written, in which at last he cried out at his tormentors, the sharpest thorn in the martyr's skin was Scotland. Scotland was the special place where he did not belong. The toffs went there in the summer and fished and hunted and knew the names of streams and glens that sounded magical to him, although and because they were forbidden. The school lesson he retained most vividly in life was not Latin, at which he excelled, nor history nor anything else found in books—it was the sharp disdainful reminder that Scotland was for aristocrats and so was no place for him. He had to attain it first before he could unleash his rage at those who had denied him.

And Jura had been recommended by David Astor, whose judgment and decency Orwell greatly respected. Though they had not known each other for long, Astor and Orwell had become close friends. They shared ideals, not background: David Astor was a member of one of the richest families in England (and, indeed, America, until his grandfather had become a British citizen). His father, Waldorf Astor (the hotel was built on the site of the family homestead in New York), was a viscount, and his mother, Nancy Astor, was the first woman ever to serve in the House of Commons. The English Astors lived at Cliveden, one of the great country houses, and for years the Cliveden set was famous for the power and celebrity of its members, as well as for supporting appeasement of Nazi Germany in the 1930s. Though this charge is disputed by some Astors, it was widespread enough to give credence to this anecdote, still making the rounds, about an exchange on the floor of the House of Commons:

LADY ASTOR: If you were my husband, Mr. Churchill,
I would put arsenic in your coffee.
WINSTON CHURCHILL: If you were my wife, madam,
I would drink it.

Astor's family owned, among many other things, *The Observer,* a major London paper. Orwell was asked to become a regular contributor, which he did. David Astor's political views were somewhat similar to Orwell's—he hated the orthodoxies of either Right or Left. And they had more in common than politics. Many of those who observed Orwell over the years made the same comment: Despite his shabby clothing, he was obviously a natural aristocrat. In terms of dignity, goodwill, dispassion, and fairness, Orwell and Astor were much the same.

But however friendly they became, however similar their nuanced sympathies in the class war, Astor still came from the very pinnacle of the world from which Orwell had been excluded at St. Cyprian's. And so, when Orwell said he wanted to get away from London and work on a new book, and when Astor then mentioned the lovely island of Jura, where his family had maintained a lodge for deer hunting, and spoke the magic word "Scotland," the ugly past that had constricted Orwell all his life opened to a peaceful place from which now Richard would be able to emerge unscathed into a better world. This seemed like the "golden country" of which he soon would write.

The house that Orwell found for Richard and himself on Jura was called Barnhill. It was large and near the sea, but had no electricity and was in very poor repair. He moved there when he should have been recuperating in a hot, dry climate.

But Jura was a good place to write. Orwell was marshaling his strength to write one last book. He needed peace and quiet, and the fame that had come with *Animal Farm* made that difficult to find in London. Most writers yearn for a lonely island, but Jura was not Bali Hai. Isolation could have been achieved with far less austerity.

It is easy to say that Jura represented a subconscious acceptance of St. Cyprian's cult of Scotland, but there are other explanations for the move. Perhaps Orwell thought the ghastly totalitarian society he was writing about might come to pass. If so, Jura would be relatively immune from Big Brother.

But Orwell's real motive in choosing Jura was probably paternal. He cared about his son and felt that a Scottish island would be a good place to raise him. And as it turned out, Jura *was* a good spot for Richard. He loved it. He thrived there. He went fishing and on picnics with his father. Orwell read him books and made toys for him.

"I liked living at Barnhill," Richard recalled years later. "It was marvelous for a child, with acres of land to roam on. Nobody minded too much where I went."

And he was not lonely. Orwell's sister Avril moved to Jura in order to help him raise the child. Susan Watson was there for the same reason. Two strong-willed women on a small island competing for control of a single child was not a recipe for harmony, and Susan soon left. It was just as well; Orwell had been hostile to her boyfriend after learning that he was a communist.

There were other children on the island, though Richard had to walk miles to play with them. He didn't mind. And there were always things to do. He accompanied his father on the daily round of farmer's chores. There was a cow to be milked, and there were goats and geese and horses and a pig, which was regarded as the family pet—until they ate it.

And there were visitors, which, given the rigors of the journey to Jura, was a tribute to the loyalty of Orwell's friends. The last thing the exhausted guests wanted on arrival was to contemplate the return journey, and so some, like Sir Richard Rees, stayed on and on. Rees, though born an aristocrat, was very close to Orwell. He was a fellow veteran of the Spanish Civil War—on the same side as his socialist friend.

(The Waughs had frequent houseguests, too. Cyril Connolly was completely unnerved by various Waugh offspring deployed by their father to continually jump out from behind hedges to shout, "Mr. Connolly, I presume.")

At Jura, the Orwells were self-sufficient. A young Scotsman named Bill Dunn, who had lost a leg in the war, joined the household to help with the farming. At this time, even though the war was over, severe rationing was still common. At Barnhill, however, there was plenty to eat. They caught lobsters off the coast and fished for salmon and trout in the lakes and streams. Orwell shot rabbits, and a large family garden helped supply the table.

But if the island was heaven for a child, it remained the last place on earth where Orwell should have been. Everyone who saw him was shocked by his appearance: "hellish," "ghastly," "haggard." Weak and exhausted, he should have been in bed, and getting the best medical treatment. The nearest hospital to Jura was in Glasgow, a long and difficult journey away, part of it over rough seas. The island's only doctor could be reached only by walking for hours. Medicine had to be ordered by mail. There was no telephone. These inconveniences took on perhaps more significance because of the fact that the island was overrun by adders. No one in the Orwell ménage seems ever to have been bitten, but everyone learned to walk very carefully.

Even when it wasn't raining, Orwell breathed little fresh air. When he was not doing chores or playing with Richard, he spent much of his time shut up in an upstairs room, writing. He knew that he had one last book in him, and he seemed by sheer will alone able to postpone death until that book was written. He lived for *1984*, and for Richard.

He wrote under the most appalling conditions. The room in which he worked was cold, and since there was no electricity, his light came from oil lamps and heat from a smoky stove. As if the air in the room was not sufficiently foul, Orwell, as he always had, chain-smoked hand-rolled cigarettes filled with strong Spanish tobacco.

It may seem that nothing could have shortened Orwell's life more surely than living on Jura and smoking one cigarette right after another as he worked all night, but through foolhardiness he managed even to increase the odds against his survival. Off the northern coast of Jura is a whirlpool so famous that it has a name, the Corryvreckan whirlpool, designated by the Royal Navy as particularly hazardous. George Orwell was less concerned. He decided one day to lead an expedition to the other side of the island and set off by motorboat with a visiting niece and nephew, then young adults, and Richard.

Orwell shrugged off warnings about the whirlpool, saying that he had carefully studied the tides. But his calculations proved to be flawed. The Orwell party sailed right into the whirlpool. The motor was ripped off the boat. They tried to row, but the boat swung about wildly. A seal popped out of the water to see what was going on. "Curious thing about seals," remarked Orwell. "Very inquisitive creatures."

At this point the boat tipped over. Orwell grabbed Richard and they all made it to a nearby island. They were cold and, of course, completely soaked. After several hours, by great good fortune, a lobster boat saw them and picked them up. The fishermen wanted to take them directly to Barnhill by traveling along the coast to the house, but Orwell, the expert on tides and seals, pooh-poohed this suggestion and insisted they just be dropped off on the nearest point of the Jura coast. So the cold, wet, and exhausted group walked four or five miles back to the farmhouse. The great wonder is that Orwell even survived the night, but the sounds of the typewriter could still be heard from his smoke-filled room.

After he finished his first draft of *1984*, Orwell finally permitted himself to be examined by a chest specialist, who had come over from Glasgow. The doctor confirmed that Orwell had tuberculosis and expressed horror at the way he had been living. The desperately sick Orwell was hospitalized near Glasgow. Seven months later, in the summer of 1948, he was allowed to return to Jura but warned not to do any work. Nevertheless, he immediately began typing the second draft of his book.

He managed to finish that draft, but the manuscript had so many handwritten corrections and changes that it was legible only to Orwell. He asked his publisher to send a typist to Jura, so they could work together to produce a readable manuscript. But the publisher could find no one willing to make the journey, so Orwell typed it over himself, averaging five thousand words a day.

Only when this was completed did he leave Jura. He never returned. He went to a sanatorium in England, at Cranham, about one hundred miles from London. He left there in 1949 for a bed in a London hospital, where he would die in January 1950. And shortly before he did die, this gaunt, gray man surprised his friends one more time: He got married. He married Sonia Brownell, an exceptionally beautiful young woman whom he had known at *Horizon* magazine years earlier. He had proposed to her (among others) shortly after Eileen's death. He must have done so again when she visited him in the hospital, and this time she accepted. The ceremony was performed in the hospital room, with the groom, forty-six, remaining in bed. The only friend of Orwell's present was David Astor, who later remarked, "Eileen was his workaday wife; Sonia was an idealized female he dreamt of. . . . It was a gesture to say he wasn't going to die." Despite his terrible physical condition, his life might have been saved by a new drug, streptomycin, that was not yet available in England. Astor managed to have some shipped from America to England, but the English doctors were insufficiently familiar with its administration to be of any help to Orwell. His tuberculosis could have been quickly cured, but instead he grew weaker and weaker, and died not long after getting married.

He wanted to live, but other than concern for Richard he had no regrets. He had lived the life he had chosen, and he had finished the book that immortalized every single lesson of that life. He hated to leave Richard and worried that his son might feel rebuffed because toward the end, the contagion of Orwell's disease had kept the two from physical closeness.

That worry was unfounded. Richard was just fine. After Orwell's death he was raised by Avril—and Bill Dunn, whom

Avril had married. He went not to Westminster, but to the same school in Scotland that Bill Dunn had attended. Richard became a farmer, married, and had two children. Since Sonia Orwell's death, he has received the steady royalties from his father's books, most particularly from the book for which his father fought off death. And Richard remembers well what was for him truly a golden country.

"It's a strange feeling having George Orwell for a father," he has said. "I can be on the outside looking in, seeing George Orwell simply as a well known figure. But I also feel that I was his son, and part of him. He was my father—there was no question about it, although I'd been adopted by him. He was my father."

ON JURA AND AT PIERS COURT, which was a kind of island, too, Orwell and Waugh had created private worlds where they lived—really lived—life with their families. They also lived life with their senses. Orwell knew the name of every plant and flower and tree he saw, because his path through life was softened by the sight of nature's effulgent offerings. Waugh knew wine as he knew his native language or his acquired faith, to be savored in order to be more fully alive, and he knew each vintage and its vineyard through taste alone, with the same gratitude that Orwell felt for the budding of a hawthorn bush. These are some of the small ways in which one truly lives a life.

CHAPTER 8

The Meeting

—

SIX MONTHS BEFORE GEORGE ORWELL DIED, WHEN HE was already terribly ill and confined to his bed in the Cotswold Sanatorium in Cranham, he received a visit from Evelyn Waugh, who lived not far away.

Had that meeting never taken place, we still would know today what they thought about each other. Though it might have seemed improbable to the loyal readership of either, the devout but sybaritic country squire and the ascetic socialist admired each other very much—each for the quality of his writing and for his moral courage.

Though they were the same age and had lived in the same city, and both were full-time writers, it is not surprising they did not meet until Orwell was dying, for they lived in different worlds. It is entirely possible that Waugh had not even heard of Orwell until 1945, the year that *Animal Farm* was published, because that is when Orwell entered the world of celebrity, which Waugh had inhabited for nearly twenty years.

You might say they were brought together by P. G. Wodehouse.

Those who have read Wodehouse will be smiling now on encountering his name, because it's impossible not to smile at the memory of his whimsical fiction. He was an enormously successful comic writer for more than seventy years. Though he was born and educated and achieved his first fame as a writer in England, and his characters, such as Bertie Wooster and his valet, Jeeves, are as quintessentially English as Alice in Wonderland, Wodehouse in fact lived for almost fifty years in France and the United States. He wrote for Hollywood and Broadway, working with Cole Porter on the musical *Anything Goes* and writing the lyrics for Jerome Kern's song "Bill" in *Show Boat*.

The comic innocence of Wodehouse's characters is a reflection of the man himself. He was like a happy child, one whose apparently effortless genius had made him rich and adored. He lived his life in a rosy bubble.

When the Germans invaded France in 1940, Wodehouse lived in a seaside villa in Le Touquet on France's northern coast. He wondered why all the other Englishmen in the neighborhood were rushing back across the channel. He was still wondering when German soldiers entered his garden and arrested him. He was interned in Upper Silesia, then part of Germany, near the Polish border. (Upon arriving there with his fellow prisoners, Wodehouse remarked, "If this is *Upper* Silesia, one must wonder what *Lower* Silesia must be like.") He was eventually released from internment and moved by the Germans into the splendid Adlon Hotel in Berlin. There he very foolishly agreed to make some radio broadcasts to America (which was not yet in the war). The five broadcasts took the form of interviews with the CBS correspondent in Berlin. The talks were droll and, from the German point of view, unhelpful. But they caused an uproar in Great Britain, where it was felt that any broadcast by an Englishman from Berlin, however innocuous, was aiding the enemy. Though in fact his only real

collaboration had been with Jerome Kern, on *Show Boat,*
Wodehouse was described as a traitor and it was suggested in
Parliament that he be tried as such.

Early in 1945, Orwell wrote a strong article titled "In Defense of P. G. Wodehouse." His calm prose reads today as an
unassailable argument that Wodehouse was guilty only of
naïveté, but saying so then took considerable courage. Wodehouse was never tried, but he did leave England forever. His
mistaken judgment, if not entirely forgiven, came to be better
understood; he was knighted shortly before his death.

One of those who admired Orwell's article was Waugh. He
regarded Wodehouse as "the Master," who could "produce on
average three uniquely brilliant and entirely original similes to
every page." Waugh owned all of Wodehouse's books and had
had them specially bound in leather. He must have been particularly pleased by Orwell's dismissal of the charge that Wodehouse in his novels caricatured a particular type—"the silly-ass
Englishman with his spats and his monocle"—and therefore
was anti-British. Orwell was stating the obvious: Wodehousian
mockery of the privileged classes was only "a mild facetious-
ness covering an unthinking acceptance." (This was, of course,
perfectly true of Waugh as well.)

Waugh had tried to defend Wodehouse, too, but he realized
his limitations in this effort. For most Englishmen, the war had
been a struggle on behalf of the common man. The privileged
classes were particularly unpopular just then, in part because
they had appeased Hitler in the years before the war, but also
because shared wartime privation had made many English un-
willing to return to the vast wealth inequities of the prewar
years. Even Churchill, the most prescient foe of the Nazis, was
thrown out of office with his fellow Conservatives at about this

time. Waugh was seen as a rich aristocrat (he was neither, but had played the role too well), and so anything he wrote on behalf of Wodehouse would surely be suspect and probably counterproductive. Orwell, on the other hand, was the quintessential man of the Left to everyone except the communists and those who heard his Eton accent. His integrity, and the life of austerity that proved it, became a cloak of honor that he shared in protecting Wodehouse. If *Orwell* supported him, then surely the charges must be absurd. When, at the start of the war, Waugh had wangled himself into battle, Orwell had praised his courage, regretting the fact that so few of those he knew on the Left had joined the battle. Now it was Waugh who was filled with admiration for Orwell for having the courage to defend Wodehouse despite the scorn of his fellow socialists.

When *Animal Farm* came out later that year, in August 1945, Orwell sent Waugh a copy. Waugh replied:

30 AUGUST 1945

Dear Mr. Orwell,

I am most grateful to you for sending me a copy of your ingenious and delightful allegory.

It was, of course, one of the books I was seeking to buy, and, of course, finding sold-out everywhere.

Yours sincerely,
Evelyn Waugh

This is the gracious note of a complete stranger. The "Mr. Orwell" means that they've never met, and perhaps even that

Waugh didn't realize that the other writer's real name was Eric Blair. The praise, however, was genuine. When someone of Waugh's celebrity writes of an "ingenious and delightful allegory," he can reasonably expect those words to appear in subsequent advertising for the book, and so he chooses each word carefully. And while Waugh was capable of wild fabrication in order to fluster or flatter a duke, he would not under torture deviate from the truth about the quality of anybody's writing. He *had* liked *Animal Farm.* As he told his diary, "I dined with my Communist cousin Claud [Cockburn] who warned me about Trotskyist literature, so that I read and greatly enjoyed Orwell's *Animal Farm.*"

So did a great many others, all over the world. And with *Animal Farm* a huge success, it was only natural for the public to wonder whether Orwell had written anything else. His publisher hurried out a collection of essays Orwell had written between 1939 and 1945. This was *Critical Essays,* reviewed by Waugh in *The Tablet,* a weekly Catholic newspaper, in April 1946.

When Waugh picked up that volume, it is likely that the only Orwell essay he had already read was the one on Wodehouse. He quickly saw that Orwell was a great writer, and, far more important in his eyes, a man to whom morality was everything. In this Waugh no doubt recognized himself. For behind the snobbery, the social climbing, the endless parties and the bottomless glasses, Waugh's life was as dedicated to moral principles as Orwell's. To Waugh, the only moral compass was the Catholic Church. Drunkenness and frivolity were of no importance, because they were little related to the life of the spirit after death. In that sense, everything in this life was irrelevant—social justice as well as debauchery. All that mattered here on earth was strict adherence to the doctrines of the true faith. Therefore, he simply couldn't understand why someone as highly moral as Orwell wasn't deeply religious, too.

An exemplary person and writer, Orwell had "one serious weakness," according to Waugh: "He has an unusually high moral sense and respect for justice and truth, but he seems never to have been touched at any point by a conception of religious thought and life." Orwell's ignorance of Catholic life kept this good man from ever getting to "the root of the matter." Orwell himself had identified the very same root of the matter—the necessary choice between this world and the next—and had chosen to improve this world. Waugh thought lasting improvement was impossible in a secular society, and that only when people truly believed in an afterlife might their behavior be modified on earth.

This was the great fundamental difference between the two men: One was concerned entirely with this world and the other with the next.

But, putting religion aside (which Waugh never did), "It remains to say that Mr. Orwell's writing is as readable as his thought is lucid. . . . There is nothing in his writing that is inconsistent with high moral principles."

Orwell was pleased by Waugh's essay, but still they did not meet. These were, after all, the Jura years, and it is difficult to imagine Waugh trudging across the soggy tundra on a nonreligious pilgrimage.

In any event, each was busy with his own work. "English writers at forty," wrote Waugh when he was forty, "either set about prophesizing, or acquiring a style. Thank God I am beginning to acquire a style." He was acquiring it in great haste. On leave from the service at a country hotel, writing furiously before being recalled to duty, producing often thousands of words a day, he captured his world and his faith in the sinuous prose of *Brideshead Revisited*.

It was different from anything he'd written before. Into it he poured, in every sense but the literal, his heart and his soul. They were not the same. His soul belonged to the church, but his heart beat for splendors and luxury now lost. Waugh knew very well that whichever side won the war, the life his class had known was over. Even if the Allies triumphed, the future would be efficient, faithless, and no damned fun.

So he set about in *Brideshead Revisited* to catalog every glittering facet of the privileged class that had finally taken him in. He was writing in the spring of 1944. Years of rationing and shortages and blockades and blackouts had transformed his England completely. The Bright Young Men were at war, and the Bright Young Women were doing war work in factories and hospitals at home. Country homes, including Waugh's beloved Piers Court, now provided refuge or schooling for city children evacuated from the blitz. Everyone was shabby, poorly nourished, and exhausted.

So in his little hotel room, Captain Waugh wrote a paean to what once had been. He wrote fervently, in a world on fire, in order to shelter in his pages all the glory of the lives that his gods had lived. He left nothing out. It was a Noah's Ark of species that were about to be extinct. Every excess was lovingly recalled—the vast country estate, a graceful palace where even the servants had servants; a great cellar whose vintages would spoil if not drunk soon; a noble mansion overlooking Green Park; a palazzo in Venice from which to glide in gondolas to costumed fetes; a first-class suite on the most luxurious liner; undergraduate Oxford as a luncheon party of plover's eggs and champagne; debauchery; languor; absolute social certitude.

And the greatest treasure in those pages is his prose. It is more silken and elegant than anything it describes. The wrapping is better than the gift. His words caress the fragments of his tale. A meal in Paris: "The cream and hot butter mingled and overflowed, separating each glaucose bead of caviar from its fellows, capping it in white and gold." Intimation of romance: "As I took the cigarette from my lips and put it in hers, I caught a thin bat's squeak of sexuality, inaudible to any but me." Explaining the disdain of a Sudanese servant for the squalor of Morocco: "For he regarded this ancient center of his culture as a New Zealander might regard Rome." Waugh at forty was certainly acquiring a style.

(When Waugh's daughter Teresa was a young woman she was introduced to Sir Max Beerbohm, perhaps the most exquisite writer of the generation before Waugh's. "Your father writes with a pen, doesn't he?" Beerbohm asked. "Yes he does," replied Teresa. "How did you know?" Beerbohm replied that such graceful phrases could not have been pounded into being on a typewriter. Orwell composed on a typewriter, and though his lucidity is unsurpassed, his prose—at least in his fiction—remains more powerful than enchanting.)

Brideshead Revisited is by far Waugh's bestselling book. Some read it only for the beauty of its language and the splendors it describes. But it is fundamentally a deeply religious novel. The baroque creation soars but is designed to house the simple expression of faith.

The point of the book is affirmation of the Catholic faith. It is more concerned with guilt than gilt. Far too many readers missed this, distracted like children in church with the glorious frescoes when they were supposed to be praying.

Just look beyond the furniture. *Brideshead Revisited* is not the usual love story. It is instead: Boy meets girl, boy loses girl, boy *deserves* to lose girl, because according to the church, they both have been living in sin. The book is narrated in the first person by Charles Ryder, a painter. He becomes entranced by several members of the Catholic and aristocratic Marchmain family. Later, though married, he falls madly in love with the Marchmains' elder daughter, Julia. She is married as well, but she abandons her husband, and he his wife and children, to live together in the fabulous Marchmain castle, Brideshead. Their love is perfect. Their house is the grandest in England. This is Waugh's view of heaven on earth.

But since Waugh also believed in heaven in heaven, this is not the end of his story. Julia's father, Lord Marchmain, returns from Italy to die at home. He is a lapsed Catholic, with no faith left at all. Indeed, he hates the church. When his son brings a priest to the sickroom, Lord Marchmain disinherits his heir and leaves the castle to Julia. So now the lovers can have everything that they (and Waugh) could wish for in this life. They can marry and spend the rest of their lives in splendor.

And then Lord Marchmain's condition worsens. He is no longer even conscious. Only a few hours of life remain. Julia, despite Charles's remonstrations, sends for a priest, who says the words of absolution to the unconscious man and anoints his forehead with oil. Family members stand around the bed and watch Lord Marchmain, who seems not even to be breathing. He stirs. All are transfixed as the unconscious man moves his hand. Slowly but unmistakably, his eyes still shut, he makes the sign of the cross. And soon after, he dies.

The rekindling of his faith returns Julia to her own. She says good-bye to Charles.

I can't marry you Charles; I can't be with you ever again. . . .

The worse I am, the more I need God. I can't shut myself out from His mercy. That is what it would mean; starting a life with you, without Him. . . . I saw today there was one thing unforgivable . . . to set up a rival good to God's. . . .

It may be a private bargain between me and God, that if I give up this one thing I want so much. . . . He won't quite despair of me in the end.

Charles never sees her again. He understands, which perhaps is more than can be said for some readers of *Brideshead Revisited*. They may have missed the point, and yet the point could not have been more plain. Julia and Charles had to part because they had been living together when not married—to each other, that is. And because they had spouses, their love was a sin in the eyes of the church. It could not be cured by obtaining divorces; the church did not recognize divorce. Even if Julia and Charles were to marry legally, they would still be living in sin in the eyes of her church.

Orwell said that we must choose between life in this world and the next. Waugh completely agreed. So he had Julia choose the next life. To have chosen happiness in this life would have been "to set up a rival good to God's."

Since both Orwell and Waugh saw this choice as, in Waugh's words, "the root of the matter" that divided them, one might have thought that Orwell would have hated *Brideshead Revisited*. But in fact he liked it a great deal. He wrote a friend that he found Waugh's new book "very good, in spite of hideous faults on the surface." These hideous faults included belief in the Catholic faith, fascination with the upper classes, and being written in the first person. But these were only "surface" faults, because Waugh was a great writer and Orwell recognized a masterwork.

The war was over and now both writers were famous. They had reached the stage of exchanging books. In early 1948, Waugh sent Orwell copies of *Black Mischief* and *A Handful of Dust*. Orwell, whose own novels prior to *Animal Farm* were hard to find, quickly had his agent send a copy of *Coming Up for Air*.

Waugh considered *Brideshead Revisited* his very best work but didn't send a copy to Orwell, correctly assuming that he had already read it. Almost everyone had. *Brideshead Revisited* was enormously successful from the start. In Britain, where austerity had survived the war, people longed to read about the good old days whose abundance few had really known but which now provided a bright glow in a world turned cold and gray.

In America, Waugh's book was even more popular. It was strongly recommended by the Catholic Church in a country with a much larger Catholic readership than Britain's. So welcome was Waugh's religious message that the clergy largely overlooked all that stuff about Charles and Sebastian in the earlier part of the book. It was, after all, not really *specific*.

But the book was a major bestseller in the states for reasons well beyond its affirmation of faith. People liked to read about the high life, and the book evoked a glamorous time. Waugh predicted that no one in America would know about or be interested in the world he re-created. If so, they certainly welcomed his introduction to it. People loved the way it was written. It is still selling, because the style Waugh acquired at forty remains an undiminished joy. And this is particularly true when he is writing not about heaven but rather describing luxury here on earth. However pure his faith, his pen often seems animated more by his heart than by his soul.

Orwell completely understood what Waugh's book was really about. In an anonymously penned review for the *Times Literary Supplement* in August 1948, Orwell defended Waugh against attacks from the poet D. S. Savage, who sneered at *Brideshead Revisited* as an example of Waugh's "immaturity." Orwell is aghast that Savage "does not even mention Mr. Waugh's conversion to Catholicism, which obviously cannot be left out of any account in any serious study of his work. In *Brideshead Revisited* Mr. Savage can see only nostalgia for adolescence, and does not seem to have noticed that the essential theme of the book is the collision between ordinary decent behavior and the Catholic concept of good and evil." Waugh would probably have agreed with this summary of the theme of his book, though he might have thought that "decent" was an unnecessary word that tipped the balance to Orwell's preference for one of those colliding concepts.

The crucial thing about how Orwell saw Waugh is that he took him seriously. What other secular critic was there, then or now, who saw the greatest issue of our time as the choice between good works in this life and belief in the hereafter? Many who believed in life after death saw this as the great moral choice, but of those who did not share that belief but still respected the choice, there seems only to have been Orwell.

Waugh saw Orwell as an innately religious man who didn't believe in religion. His lack of faith led him to choose this world over the next, and he then spent—indeed sacrificed—his life in the effort to improve it. From Waugh's perspective, that time was largely wasted. No one could improve this world because people no longer had faith, and therefore only chaos was possible.

Orwell understood exactly where Waugh was coming from, but he wasn't going there. It would have meant giving up *politics*. And to him everything in this world was political, just as everything in Waugh's world was related to faith. Politics for Orwell had little to do with winning elections—it was the day-to-day struggle against injustice; for him, belief in the next life was just an excuse for inaction in this one.

When Waugh wrote a short comic novel, *Scott-King's Modern Europe*, Orwell reviewed it for the front page of *The New York Times Book Review* (one indication of his heightened visibility since the success of *Animal Farm*). The novel is slight not only in length; it is one of Waugh's lesser works. It's the picaresque tale of an English classics professor who goes to a postwar conference in the right-wing Republic of Neutralia, which is ruled by a marshal and bears some resemblance to Tito's Yugoslavia. The guests at the conference are pawns of the vile marshal, and Scott-King is lucky to escape alive.

Orwell's review of this slight farce is largely political. And he claims that Waugh, in his way, is political, too, at least in his moral basis for disengagement with the present: "The modern world, we are meant to infer, is so unmistakably crazy, so certain to smash itself to pieces in the near future, that to attempt to understand it or come to terms with it is simply a purposeless self-corruption. In the chaos that is shortly coming, a few moral principles that one can cling to . . . will be more useful than what is now called 'enlightenment.' "

Orwell thus sums up Waugh's philosophy so precisely that for a moment he almost switches sides: "There is something to be said for this point of view." And then, pulling himself away from temptation and back to the barricades, he unintentionally gives us a good example of why Waugh could see all politics as futile. He complains that Waugh should never have suggested that evil Neutralia was a right-wing dictatorship. He should have made it a *left*-wing dictatorship, which in Orwell's view it most resembles. He complains that this sort of sloppiness in political attribution suggests "there is nothing to choose between communism and fascism." But that's pretty much what Waugh believed. And to some extent what Orwell believed, too. By the end of *Animal Farm* you couldn't tell the pigs from the humans. They had become the same.

WHETHER OR NOT HE ACCEPTED Waugh's heaven, Orwell was at peace. He had finished the great work of his life. Orwell's *1984* was his epiphany as surely as *Brideshead Revisited* was Waugh's. Everything he felt about the world was in it.

Because *1984* is now so well-known, so completely integrated into our culture, it is hard to imagine how startling it must have seemed when it was published in 1949. Many may have thought it was science fiction, which was becoming quite popular at the time. The very title, after all, proclaims that the story takes place in the future. The first sentence in the book describes an altered world: The clocks are striking thirteen.

But then something seems wrong. The future was supposed to be clean and efficient. Everything in this future is dirty or broken. Nothing works except the people, and their labor is involuntary. There is no privacy. Television sets watch everyone. The slightest deviation from loyalty to the head of state, Big Brother, is reported by friends or family. The world is continuously at war. Language has been deliberately perverted to prevent clear speech—and clear thought. There is no point to life save blind worship of the state—no love, no thought, no nature, no beauty—and, most important of all, no past.

Objective reality has been abolished. Nothing exists except the constantly changing version of events as described by the state. There are no ancient truths; there is not even any current truth. "Reality" changes at the whim and need of Big Brother.

Orwell's main character, Winston Smith, is a technocrat trained to alter every record of what really happened. Something tells him that what he is doing is wrong. His enlightenment comes not from intellect but from instinct. The mind can be trained to conform, but there remains in humans, however buried, an inherent insistence on *being* human, free to act in a world of objective truth in which two plus two always equals four.

Winston falls in love with a young woman, Julia, who shares his hatred of their oppressors. The only possible forms of rebellion are love and sex, since these are personal and beyond the state. Their romance is discovered. They are tortured so brutally that the spark of humanity is snuffed out. Winston no longer can love Julia; he now believes that two plus two equals five—or whatever else the state says.

This book was written at a time in which most intellectuals believed the state could expand human freedom. Orwell's message was just the opposite. To a remarkable extent, he changed the future by describing it to a vast global audience.

His magnum opus now complete, Orwell continued his correspondence and published a number of reviews. And he set about to write a major essay on Evelyn Waugh.

Philip Rahv, the editor of *Partisan Review* in New York,

asked Orwell in February 1949 to write a long piece on Waugh for his magazine. Orwell agreed, and though he was bedridden in Cranham, set out at once to read those words of Waugh he had missed, starting with Waugh's earliest book, on Rossetti.

Orwell never finished his essay on Waugh. He was simply too sick. He abandoned the task in April, having read a number of Waugh's books and actually having written the beginning part of the essay. That this dying man could even read, let alone write, was amazing. But he wrote as well as ever. The fragment of his essay remains. Though extraordinarily lucid, it adds little but nuance to what Orwell already had written about Waugh.

It does, however, include a warning about the new class of educated but rootless people that was arising in the postwar world, and its fierce enforcement of political correctness. "Within the last few decades, in countries like Britain or the United States, the literary intelligentsia has grown large enough to constitute a world in itself. One important result of this is that the opinions which a writer feels frightened of expressing are not those which are disapproved of by society as a whole."

Orwell states this in order to praise Waugh as the exception. "In our own day, the English novelist who has most conspicuously defied his contemporaries is Evelyn Waugh. . . . In the whole of [his] age-group, the only loudly discordant voice was Waugh's."

This is not quite correct. There was one other loudly discordant voice from someone almost exactly the same age: Orwell himself. He wasn't a conservative, like Waugh, but was something even less acceptable to the orthodoxy of the Left: an outspoken anticommunist. He had suffered for this honesty all his life, even more so than Waugh. To Orwell, no virtue was greater than unpopular dissent. He was right to honor Waugh in this regard, and quite in character not to name—perhaps not even to think of naming—himself.

In his final essay, Orwell describes his view of Waugh's writing one last time. "Though the approach is at the level of farce, the essential theme is serious. What Waugh is trying to do is to use the feverish, cultureless modern world as a set-off for his own conception of a good and stable way of life." Waugh's novels "are really sermons in farcical shape."

That's about it. The essay had to be abandoned before Orwell could take up the subject of *Brideshead Revisited,* only mentioning that the book "perhaps indicates a new departure" for Waugh. Orwell was too sick to follow up on this, but his discussion of *Brideshead Revisited* in the *Times Literary Supplement* less than a year earlier tells us what he might have said.

And there is one last thing about the essay fragment. No first-class writer could have read *Brideshead Revisited* without awe, if not envy, for the triumph of its style. Orwell was a first-class writer. In his adumbrated essay he engages in the sincerest form of flattery—he tries to write in Waugh's style. In describing the look of the typical English country house, he writes of "the walled garden with its crucified pear-trees."

Orwell also left some handwritten notes for the unfinished essay. One note refers to *Brideshead Revisited:*

Last scene, where the unconscious man makes the sign of the Cross. . . . One cannot really be Catholic & grown up. . . .

Conclude. Waugh is about as good a novelist as one can be . . . while holding untenable opinions.

The finished essay might well have gone on to say that Waugh was a great novelist, period. Orwell shared with his close friend and fellow journalist T. R. Fyvel what he intended to write about Waugh, and Fyvel has left us a record of their conversation:

> I recall him saying something like "The point about Evelyn Waugh is that he disproves the Marxist theory that a worthwhile writer has to be in tune with the basic political and economic trends of his age." Waugh wrote about an imagined English landed aristocracy which in the real world had long abdicated from true social leadership. Even so, said Orwell, for all that they held opposed political viewpoints, Waugh was the best English writer of his generation. . . .
>
> I think it a great pity that this essay was never written.

So do we all. But we do have its fragment, as well as notes and other writing and comments by Orwell on Waugh. We can see that he sensed how much Waugh was like himself not only in courage but philosophy. He would have honored him.

Though no longer able to write, the frail and dying Orwell had become globally famous. After being published in June 1949, *1984* became a sensation and has remained remarkably popular ever since, selling more than fifty million copies. It fomented the intellectual implosion of totalitarianism. It gave the English language the word "Orwellian," which helps greatly to puncture the gasbags of verbal deceit. It gives hope to the subjected and clarity to the guardians of freedom. Today, in the harsh dictatorship of Burma (now known as Myanmar), the country that young Eric Blair once helped to police, *1984* is banned by law, but tattered copies are taken from their hiding places and shared. The Burmese know it describes a world in which the people are chained, a world much like their country, and that this small book has already helped to free other such worlds. Perhaps their turn will come.

The man who had endured a life of privation in the service of his writing was too weak to enjoy the riches and fame his perseverance had brought him at last. He would be dead in six months. He was confined to a hospital bed. His typewriter had been taken away, a modern variant on bleeding the patient to death in a misguided effort to help him. He did manage to hide a bottle of rum under the bed and continued to chain-smoke whenever he could get away with it, acts as defiant and foolhardy as steering into the Corryvreckan whirlpool off Jura.

He could still read, though, and must have been gratified by all the letters of praise for *1984*. One of them was from Evelyn Waugh, written on July 17, 1949, to Orwell in the Cranham Sanatorium. It is a remarkable document.

By this time he, and everyone else in the literary world, knew Orwell's real name. "Dear Orwell—Blair—which do your prefer?" the letter begins.

The opening lines are devoted to the theme of homage well earned. "I have seen a number of reviews, English & American, all respectful and appreciative. I won't repeat what they say. Please believe that I echo their admiration for your ingenuity and for many parts of the writing, e.g. the delicious conversation in the pub when Winston tries to pump the old man for memories of pre-revolution days."

He then proceeded to his real point.

But the book failed to make my flesh creep as presumably you intended. . . .

Winston's rebellion was false. His "Brotherhood" (whether real or imaginary) was simply another gang like the Party. And it was false, to me, that the form of his revolt should simply be fucking in the style of Lady Chatterley—finding reality through a sort of mystical union with the Proles in the sexual act.

In other words, the answer is never political, because one form of politics is or will become as bad as another. What, then, does matter?

"I think it possible that in 1984 we shall be living in conditions rather like those you show," Waugh writes. And then comes the real point of the letter.

But what makes your version spurious to me is the disappearance of the Church. I wrote of you once that you seemed unaware of its existence now when it is everywhere manifest. Disregard all the supernatural implications if you like, but you must admit its unique character as a social & historical institution. I believe it is inextinguishable, though of course it can be extinguished in a certain place for a certain time. The descendants of Xavier's converts in Japan kept their faith going for three hundred years and were found saying "Ave Marias" and "Pater Nosters" when the country was opened in the last century.

The Brotherhood which can confound the Party is one of love—not adultery in Berkshire, still less throw-

ing vitriol in children's faces. And men who love a crucified God need never think of torture as all-powerful.

Waugh makes, as strongly as language permits, the Catholic
case for the futility of political power when compared to that of
faith. Winston Smith did not prevail, but the patient Japanese
converts had done so, their prayers more enduring than mani-
festos. Orwell would probably have argued that closet Christianity in Japan would be impossible in a modern totalitarian
state that could alter people's thoughts.

But the difference between them was even more fundamental. They were two highly moral men confronting evil in their
world. They differed on what to do about it. It was to be or not
to be. Orwell chose to be—to take action here and now. Waugh
chose not to be in this life other than to live morally enough to
be welcomed in the next.

We'll never know exactly what Orwell thought of Waugh's
letter. Perhaps he merely put it down and reached for that bottle of rum beneath the bed.

But we do know that the letter made him want to meet its
author, because in the last paragraph Waugh asks if he might
visit, and Orwell, who could easily have begged off for reasons
of health, must have agreed to let him come.

Waugh's last paragraph is very cunningly written:

You see how much your book excited me, that I risk
preaching a sermon. I do not want to annoy you—for
one reason I have promised neighbours of mine Jack &
Frankie Donaldson (Etonian socialist farmer and Freddie Lonsdale's daughter) that I will take them to visit
you. They are earnest students of all your work and a

charming couple and I don't want to deprive them of
their treat by any sectarian zeal. Would we be welcome
one afternoon?

Yours sincerely,
Evelyn Waugh

Waugh was asking not that *he* be allowed to visit, but rather
to be permitted to bring the Donaldsons. He had *promised* the
Donaldsons. This request was structured as an offer that could
not be refused. And, to sweeten the bid, Waugh drops three
words, "Etonian socialist farmer," which were intended to appeal in ascending order to Orwell's innate loyalties. The words
were accurate, though Jack Donaldson was more Waugh's idea
of a farmer than Orwell's—he later became minister for the
arts and ended his life as a peer.

And so it was that in the late summer of 1949, before he was
moved from the Cranham Sanatorium to the London hospital
room he would never leave, Orwell received a visit from Evelyn Waugh. It was the only time the two met.

The Donaldsons, as promised, were there as well. They may
well have been included quite apart from serving as an effective
foot in the door. Waugh, despite a lifetime of outrageous cur-
mudgeonly behavior, was capable of great personal kindness.
Acutely sensitive, he may have worried about the effect of his
appearance alone at the bedside of the stricken Orwell, who was,
after all, an atheist. The sight of the embodiment of faith and
privilege all by himself, unaccompanied, might seem to Orwell
the Ghost of Christmas Future. Waugh wanted to comfort the
patient, not finish him off. So he brought the socialist Donald-

sons with him as tangible proof perhaps that he did not see Orwell as Lord Marchmain and that no deathbed conversion was being sought.

Waugh had no agenda. The one-prominent-man-of-letters-to-another thing was not his style. The visit was never publicized. Waugh likely went to see the dying Orwell because he greatly admired him and wanted to meet him while there was still time. And of course one of the corporal works of mercy for Catholics is tending the sick.

What did the two men talk about? We do not know. Orwell was too sick to keep a diary that year. Although Waugh was a dedicated diarist and maintained an active correspondence with a number of friends, there is no mention anywhere of his meeting with Orwell. In his letters he loved to drop names but never dropped this one, despite the fact it had just acquired superstar celebrity and Waugh knew that few of his own friends had met Orwell and were bound to be impressed that he had. The visit appears to have been purely personal. For Waugh saw Orwell not as another point on the scoreboard, but as his equal.

He did mention to his friend Malcolm Muggeridge that he had found Orwell "very near to God." This may mean that Orwell was obviously close to death; it may also mean Waugh thought him to be saintly. Muggeridge, in any event, found Waugh's visit amusing. In a subsequent article he said, "I should have loved to see them together: Complementary figures . . . [Waugh's] country gentleman's outfit and Orwell's proletarian one and the both out of the pages of *Punch*."

He was wrong. They were not Laurel and Hardy. They were not Leon Trotsky and Colonel Blimp. They were not the political essayist and the writer of comic novels. They were not a remnant of the past and a seer of the future. They were at the opposite ends of a spectrum, which for them—through shared morality—had become a circle, and so had brought them close. They shared the same roots, and they saw the same root in the meaning of life. And in that way, they were very much the same man.

CHAPTER 9

The Same Man

—

"AT FIFTY," GEORGE ORWELL OBSERVED, "EVERYONE HAS the face he deserves."

This was pure Orwell: a big thought in a simple phrase, not an ounce of fat in the prose, original, powerful, and, for quite a few readers, more than a little upsetting.

Many people don't *like* the face they are stuck with at fifty. No one looks as good in a photograph as in a mirror.

We cannot know with absolute certainty whether Orwell would have had the face he deserved—he didn't live to fifty. Shortly after writing that sentence, which was the final entry in his diary, he died at age forty-six, in 1950.

In photographs, of which there are not many, his face, which looked old even ten years before his death, reflects not only a life but a type—a type all too familiar in this century, the intellectual as activist, cut off from worldly pleasures, ascetic, wholly engaged. He looks poor and undernourished, but no one would mistake him for a workingman. He *looks* like an Etonian who has renounced all worldly goods.

He looks stark. As spare as his prose, the gaunt face is lined with fissures, deep wrinkles of cogitation and concern. Only his eyes, "his sad earnest eyes," as Harold Acton called them, betrayed the real person, a calm and moral gentleman.

His clothes make up for this betrayal. More stereotypical even than the face, they are the uniform of the basement pamphleteer: dark shirt, darker tie, ill-fitting jacket of coarsely woven wool, pants that never again will hold a crease.

Next we look at a photograph of Evelyn Waugh. There are many of them to choose from, for his fame came early. But Waugh did reach fifty, and the photographs show us how he looked at that age.

His face is the opposite of Orwell's. The first word that comes to mind is "florid." (Indeed, the coatroom attendant at the Ritz, where Waugh dined and drank often, could not remember this guest's name, and so wrote "florid" on the tag he stuck on Waugh's hat so he would be able to recognize its owner.) But "florid," however apt, is insufficient. Other words shove to get in line: prosperous, confidant, pompous, arrogant, cruel. Harold Acton, a much better friend of Waugh's than of Orwell's, would not have called his eyes either sad or earnest. Waugh's eyes are less like pools than buttons; they shine, they show no depth, they are like shark's eyes. (There are videotapes of him as well, and they are more revealing; we see that his eyes are, in fact, sensitive and reveal a surprising vulnerability.)

At fifty, Waugh was photographed holding a cigar like a scepter, and dressed like a lord. He looks sleek, corpulent, and assured. His gold watch chain seems a badge of office.

Even more striking pictures were taken only a few years later, at Waugh's country estate. Whether they show the face that Waugh deserves, they certainly capture the persona by which he is remembered, and, more important, the man whom he worked so carefully to resemble.

He is the country squire beyond parody. The opaque eyes glint as if from madness. Puffed-up, scornful, isolated from modernity by disdain, Waugh is clad in a suit so improbable that even his peers must have been awed by his audacity. Of his own design, the bold checkered garment could pass for a game board.

If Orwell was right about faces at fifty, then never were two men less alike. But he was not right. Perhaps when their fifth decade ends some have the face not that they deserve but that they have willed. Orwell and Waugh willed what they became. In a modern phrase that each would have hated, they invented themselves, carefully constructing public lives that could not have seemed less similar.

But even those invented lives cannot conceal the fact that Orwell and Waugh were not really opposites at all. And this is why we must view their lives together, because in the things that really matter—the moral core of each—they were very much the same man. They saw the world through the same eyes, and whether those eyes were sad or masked is of little consequence, for their vision was shared, and not only in its clarity.

What they had most in common was a hatred of moral relativism. They both believed that morality is absolute, though they defined and applied it differently. But each believed with all his heart, brain, and soul that there were such things as moral right and moral wrong, and that these were not subject to changes in fashion. Moral relativism was, in fact, the gravest of sins. Everything else they believed in common flowed from this basic perception.

Even their seemingly opposite lives were dedicated to the same cause: fighting against the future. They both saw clearly that what was coming would be worse than what was now, understanding that the dictators of their own time were harbingers of a world unlinked to faith or tradition or common sense or decency. They saw that stunted thought and pointless lives would not be redeemed merely by the military defeat of the thugs who benefited from modernity by seeming to oppose it, who used the most up-to-date techniques of propaganda and surveillance to substitute rigid conformity for the dislocations and rapid change that accompany free markets and free states.

These writers saw not only their own time, but ours. They fought the dictators, of course, but both knew that the larger battles were yet to come, and that victory over the advance scouting parties of soulless uniformity was only a first step. The real war against the future would have to be taken to the heart of the enemy camp, which was neither Moscow nor Berlin but the salons of educated but powerless fools in the democracies, where hatred of merit was packaged as disdain for absolute morality. "The common people," Orwell wrote, "are still living in the world of absolute good and evil from which the intellectuals have long since escaped."

Orwell and Waugh both feared the future because they correctly saw the evil of their own time not as throwback but preface. They both understood that moral relativism had brought the dictators to power and would outlive their regimes.

If we look at their world, we will understand what they foresaw in ours. For in the time of Orwell and Waugh there were two dictators, Hitler and Stalin, both so preternaturally evil, each a murderer on a scale beyond precedent in human history, that one finds it hard to see how Englishmen at that time could even imagine that such monsters existed outside of nightmare or fiction.

Most of the people in England shared this disbelief. It made them more vulnerable but also affirmed their sanity. To good people, anchored in a tradition of civility, it *should* be hard to imagine absolute evil or even recognize it when it appears.

The reaction of the educated classes, however, was not like this at all. There was instead division over which dictator was the better to support. The wealthy classes so feared the communist Stalin, that they accepted, with varying degree of enthusiasm, the advent of Hitler. The less wealthy members of the educated classes, from which most of the intellectuals emerged, tended to see Stalin as a bulwark against Fascism, and quite often as the hopeful augury of a more just future for the world.

In the slightly overlapping worlds in which they lived, Orwell and Waugh were among the relative handful who opposed both Hitler and Stalin. They opposed *totalitarianism*, period, and they opposed it with all their hearts. Waugh was, to be sure, a particularly archaic Tory, and Orwell a dedicated socialist, but that was merely how they voted (if Waugh indeed ever voted). What both *believed*—their core, who they were—was that individual freedom mattered more than anything else on earth and reliance on tradition was the best way to maintain it.

This separated them from most of those with whom they were in daily contact, but that did not matter. They did not live their lives for other people's approval. Yes, Waugh fought to be accepted by the upper reaches of society, because he thought that was where he belonged, but he didn't flatter to get there; he dazzled and he bludgeoned. And there were no class distinctions in his manners; he was uniformly rude to everyone he met, whether duke or gardener.

Orwell paid a terrible price for his failure to conform to the political correctness of the Left. His fervent anticommunism made him a pariah to many of his fellow socialists, and crippled his career. His poverty was not entirely a matter of choice; his politics played a role, too, or, rather, his *lack* of politics—his independence, his objectivity, his refusal to use the trendy bromides that won lucrative writing assignments for mediocrities.

Orwell was kept from publication in England because he was an anticommunist. But what about Waugh? Wasn't he a strong anticommunist, too? Yes, he was, but it didn't hamper his career because he was a humorist, and the political correctness gang was so essentially humorless they failed to take him seriously. Besides, extremists hate their apostates more than their opposites. And Waugh used his network, starting with his Oxford friends and not excluding his own derided father, to find his way into print. Orwell eschewed such connections, and the publisher he did seek didn't think he was reliably enough on the left.

Both Hitler and Stalin are long gone now, the bunker bombed, the wall pulled down. The only two choices thought viable by so many educated Englishmen in the 1930s no longer exist—not as governments, not as theories, not as threats, and certainly not as hopes to which any thinker still clings.

But the war that Orwell and Waugh fought as allies still rages on, for it was not only a war against dictators—it was a war against modernity as well. In Waugh's great World War II *Sword of Honour* trilogy "the enemy at last was plain in view. . . . It was the Modern Age in arms." He did not mean the age of Hitler or Stalin. He meant the *Modern Age*, the future we're living in now. And Orwell was his comrade in arms.

And just what is so terrible about our time? In many ways it is a better time, with more opportunity for more people than ever before. The British Empire, which Orwell hated as resting on coolie labor, is gone. The grim poverty of the average person has been substantially vanquished in the Western world and much alleviated elsewhere. Destiny is no longer determined exclusively by birth, and merit is rewarded far more often, if still imperfectly, than heretofore.

Material abundance is vastly greater and much more widely (though unequally) shared than ever in history. Poverty and starvation still exist, and plagues are potentially more lethal through the increased interconnectedness of populations, but generally speaking the ease and length of life for most people is amazingly improved since the time of Orwell and Waugh. In the places they knew best, England, Europe, and America, material comfort and nutrition for most people are superior to that enjoyed even by aristocrats back then. The Chinese are buying cars and air conditioners. India is already a major player in the Internet century. In America, a working class once gaunt is now obese.

So: The world is healthier and wealthier than ever before, and everyone agrees that it's becoming more so. The future seems to be an escalator, going up.

But not to Orwell or to Waugh. Their writing makes it clear they would dread and abhor much about our time, and might even see it as worse than their own.

Their most fundamental concern was that the Modern Age would strip humans of their humanity. They felt that man does not live by bread alone, and that the Modern Age would provide us exclusively with bread.

And circuses.

The writer who really got the Modern Age down cold was neither Orwell nor Waugh. It was Aldous Huxley. Orwell's *1984* is twenty times the book that Huxley's *Brave New World* is, but in terms of predicting what was coming, Huxley clearly was closer to getting it right. (Of course, one of the reasons *1984* wasn't better prophecy was that it was so good—so powerful it helped prevent the future it described.) *1984* foretold what it would be like if Russia won the cold war; *Brave New World* described the future if the West did. And, of course, the West did, and Huxley's 1932 satire has proved amazingly prescient. If not a flawless mirror of our time, it reflects all too clearly the paucity of our supposedly rich lives.

This is not a book about Aldous Huxley. It is about Orwell and Waugh, and how they shared the same fear about what the twenty-first century would bring. They *sensed* what was going to happen, and they sensed it correctly. But Huxley, writing even before they did, was able not just to sense but quite accurately to see just what was going to happen. We look now at *Brave New World* because it spells out, though in exaggerated form, the least admirable details of many people's lives today, from addictive video games to the decline of the family. The outlines, if not the specifics, of our lives were foreseen by Orwell and Waugh as well. They knew that the loss of tradition and civility and community and, yes, the easing of the struggle for existence, too, would lead us to a time of tranquilized conformity, though Orwell's early death and Waugh's emphasis on faith kept them from a sharper focus on the hedonism both knew would follow the dictators.

In Huxley's future, hedonism is everything, immediate pleasure the entire point of life. The only concern people have is over aging, because this life is all there is—ever. There is no religion other than gratitude to what was then called capitalism and today is referred to as free-market globalism (so as not to embarrass the Chinese). There is no tradition. No past, no future. Life is now. In fact, that's all life is—the pleasures of right now. In Huxley's future, the literature of the past has been put away—why upset people with tales of suffering? There *is* no suffering.

Huxley's point, of course, is that there is no life, either. One of his characters is the Savage, born of new-age parents but raised among a primitive tribe with access to the works of Shakespeare. As a young man he is "rescued" and returned to utopia, where he is regarded as a freak. Since his standards are Shakespeare's (and those of Orwell and Waugh, and for that matter, Huxley, a humanist who had taught Blair at Eton), he is horrified by the lack of a moral code, by the incessant pursuit of pleasure, the absence of family, or love, or connection to anything other than the sensation of the moment. The not-very-subtle point is that it's better to be a savage who loves Shakespeare than a clean and (medicatedly) calmer hedonist whose life has no meaning.

This growing displacement of all values in life by materialism and escapist pleasure was the first big problem that Orwell and Waugh feared in the Modern Age, and who, outside North Korea, would doubt how far along that road we've already gone? For many people the only reality is reality shows, which they compulsively TiVo. Who needs *Macbeth*?

The problem is not that entertainment has corrupted modern life, but somewhat the reverse: Our diversions lack content because our lives do as well. A society rich in goods but devoid of values can continually improve the quality of its toys but cannot invent escape from emptiness.

Another danger both Orwell and Waugh saw in the Modern Age is the stratification of society. Today, it is much different than in the past. Both Orwell and Waugh were products of a rigid class system. Orwell hated it, and Waugh bounded up its steps. It was an unfair system in which privilege was hereditary.

The son of a laborer would always be a laborer, and the son of a peer a peer. To an extent difficult even to comprehend now, only seventy or eighty years later, the ability of the individual was unrelated to his or her station in life. Orwell raged about this, and Waugh saw the unfairness just as acutely—some of his funniest passages deal with the bumbling inanity of the upper classes, the undeserving rich. He liked being with the aristocrats because he found their lifestyle attractive, but he knew the world was unjust. He just accepted that unfairness, because, after all, only heaven mattered.

But they both saw, just as clearly, that the future would not bring an end to class division, but would merely substitute a different set of classes. The stratification of society was unavoidable. Whichever class overthrew the upper class would become a new upper class itself, keeping everyone else in subservience.

This is stated frankly in *1984*. Orwell's central character, Winston Smith, gets a copy of the forbidden text of Emmanuel Goldstein, the Trotsky-like scapegoat of Big Brother. The first paragraph of its first chapter sets out the way the world really works:

> Throughout recorded time, and probably since the end of the Neolithic Age, there have been three kinds of people in the world, the High, the Middle, and the Low. They have been subdivided in many ways, they have borne countless different names, and their relative numbers, as well as their attitude toward one another, have varied from age to age; but the essential structure of society has never altered. Even after enormous upheavals and seemingly irrevocable changes, the same pattern has

always reasserted itself, just as a gyroscope will always return to equilibrium, however far it is pushed one way or the other.

The aims of these three groups are entirely irreconcilable. The aim of the High is to remain where they are. The aim of the Middle is to change places with the High. The aim of the Low is to abolish all distinctions.

Both Orwell and Waugh believed this to be an obvious truth. In their own time, the High class was composed of aristocrats and the very rich. The Middle that wanted to take its place was what in our own time is charitably called "the meritocracy." Orwell and Waugh both hated this new class.

It's not so surprising that Waugh was scornful of a new class based on testable skills—this was a threat to his beloved aristocracy. In the first part of *Brideshead Revisited*, his central character, Charles Ryder, patterned considerably after Waugh himself, is an officer in the Second World War whose adjutant, Hooper, is what some then called a "new man," who had risen from working-class roots to a somewhat higher station through (probably technical) ability. He is earnest, polite, and hard-working, but Waugh treats him derisively because he lacks the manner of the highly born. This seems like a flaw in an otherwise enchanting book, a lapse based purely on snobbery.

Perhaps it was, but Orwell, at about the same time, wrote with even greater hostility to the new class he also saw rising. In an essay on the American writer James Burnham, Orwell castigates those, in America as well as in England, who are sympathetic to the cruel Russian dictatorship entirely because "of the power worship now so prevalent among intellectuals." He describes this new class precisely: "They are not managers

in the narrow sense, but scientists, technicians, teachers, journalists, broadcasters, bureaucrats, professional politicians: in
general, middling people who feel themselves cramped by a
system that is still partly aristocratic, and are hungry for more
power and more prestige."

Orwell and Waugh felt that merit should not be stifled by
caste, but they saw very clearly that a society based on test-
score "merit," once it had displaced the old High class, would
be just as contemptuous of the Middle and Low classes as the
old peerage had been. This realization came later to Orwell and
must have been particularly embittering. He had written hopefully for years about the emergence of a new meritocracy; at
first he had seen it as "classless," a democratic alternative to
stratified privilege, but his vision trumped his hopes, and he
came to see, as Goldstein's words—written by Orwell at the
end of his life—cynically summarize, that class division would
always be with us, and that the emergence of a new class, even
one based on merit, would only seek to replace the aristocrats
and not abolish their supremacy.

This, of course, has happened. Much of the anger and polar-
ization in our current politics reflects the growing dominance of
a new elite and the reaction of both rich and poor against it.

In the time of Orwell and Waugh, higher education was limited to relatively few. Even in the United States then only
5 percent of the population received college degrees, but that limited access changed quickly throughout the Western world after
the Second World War. Millions of young people from working-
class backgrounds were able to earn college and postgraduate degrees. And earn them they did, as the rising tide of applicants
necessitated the lock and dam system of academic testing to control access to the limited number of classroom seats.

It was a great advance in human history that large numbers of people were no longer fettered by birth to work that did not fully utilize their interests or talent, but even good news brings unintended consequences. Increased accessibility to higher education produced a new class—in Orwell's phrase a new Middle anxious to displace the old High. Indeed, many members of the new educated class felt they were *entitled* to be the High— their superiority had been certified by test scores.

But they were disappointed to find that status and power were linked to money, and that comfortable professional incomes were no match for the treasure to be won in the marketplace. It didn't seem fair to them. Why should those C students own Bentleys? Resentment of the rich and of business in general was characteristic of much of this new class, as was contempt for the Low—their own parents, often embarrassingly ill-spoken, among them.

Over time, the Middle class did become at least part of the High class. Influential positions went to graduates of the elite schools, as before, but now those students were not there because their grandparents had been, but rather because their SATs had been high. The New Boy Network turned out to work precisely like the Old.

A perfect example of the exclusionary arrogance of any class that becomes the High is seen in Kazuo Ishiguro's Booker Prize–winning novel, *The Remains of the Day,* which was also made into a fine film. It is the story of a butler who works for one of the great aristocrats, Lord Darlington, at his palatial country home in the 1930s. Lord Darlington and his friends, no doubt all Etonians, are sympathetic to Nazi Germany and highly supportive of British appeasement of it. In this endeavor they are frustrated by the Middle (intellectuals, who prefer

Stalin) and the Low (the common people of England, who don't like any dictatorships).

Late one night the butler, Stevens, is summoned to the drawing room, where three of Lord Darlington's friends wish to question him.

"My good man," says one black-tied guest, "we need your help on a certain matter we've been debating. Tell me, do you suppose the debt situation regarding America is a significant factor in the present low levels of trade? Or do you suppose this is a red herring and that the abandonment of the gold standard is at the root of the matter?"

Stevens doesn't know what to say. "I'm very sorry, sir," he replies quite honestly, "but I am unable to be of assistance on this matter."

This does not stop the inquisition.

"Then perhaps you will help us on another matter. Would you say that the currency problem in Europe would be made better or worse if there were to be an arms agreement between the French and the Bolsheviks?"

"I'm very sorry, sir, but I am unable to be of assistance on this matter."

He is questioned further, with the same result. Finally the guest announces to his friends, with the butler still there, the point of his little quiz, which is that it is absurd "that this nation's decisions be left in the hands of our good man here and to the few million others like him. Is it any wonder, saddled as we are with our present parliamentary system, that we are unable to find any solution to our many difficulties?"

Everyone laughs, and only then is Stevens permitted to leave.

It is impossible not to be angered at this passage. The condescension is disgusting. The arrogance, the certitude about their own capacity to decide, is based on the possession of some pseudo-significant data and not real perception at all. These men are, after all, supporters of Adolf Hitler, if somewhat indirectly. They think that they, and certainly not the majority of their fellow citizens, are entitled to make all decisions regarding the fate of the country.

It is not difficult to imagine exactly the same sort of conversation taking place today, only instead of languid lords in dinner jackets, the interrogators would be members of the new elite class, certified not by birth but by diploma. They would be more casually dressed, but every bit as arrogant as Lord Darlington's guests. Perhaps more arrogant, because they believe their superiority has been "proved" by test scores. But can intelligence be quantified? It was, after all, the harbingers of the new class, "the Best and the Brightest," who sent us to war in Vietnam, an act of folly right up there with the appeasers of the 1930s. It's easy to focus on the college grades of presidents, but presidents have advisers, and the architects of disastrous follies often have the highest possible academic credentials.

The arrogance of the new elite tolerates no dissent. It was clear to both Orwell and Waugh that the new class possessed a pathological need for conformity. Modern intellectuals (Orwell called them "intellectuals," though many were not and he most certainly was) seemed particularly anxious not to step on the cracks of political correctness. "A modern literary intellectual lives and writes in constant dread—not, indeed, of public opinion in the wider sense, but of public opinion within his own group," Orwell wrote.

In our own time, political correctness is a hateful virus that has infected millions. It's a way of governing without having enough votes to pass laws, and it's partly the result of talking only to the same people. In the 1930s, it was possible for small cliques of writers to attain this insularity, but today there is so much self-segregation by educational status that the politically correct are no longer a select little club. And with the ubiquity of niche broadcasting, no one has to hear or see anything with which they're not already in agreement. The conformity of the 1930s was rooted in the ideological battles of two foreign dictatorships, but what we have today is worse—the mental goose-stepping of tens of millions on a voluntary basis. Puppets, even though no government is any longer pulling strings. Conformity based entirely on class solidarity and ignorance of anyone outside it.

Orwell came to see political correctness not as a nuisance but a danger, the substitute for law and morality in an increasingly permissive society. He would have equated our Age of Aquarius with Fascism. He felt that the code of its precursors in his own time "illustrates very well the totalitarian tendency which is implicit in the anarchist or pacifist vision of society. In a society in which there is no law, and in theory no compulsion, the only arbiter of behavior is public opinion. But public opinion because of the tremendous urge to conformity in gregarious animals, is less tolerant than any system of law. When human beings are governed by 'thou shall not,' the individual can practice a certain amount of eccentricity: when they are supposedly governed by 'love' or 'reason,' he is under continuous pressure to make him behave and think in exactly the same way as everyone else."

Orwell and Waugh defended not only the right but the willingness to say unpopular things. Defending P. G. Wodehouse for his German broadcasts was an unpopular thing to do, and when egalitarianism became the accepted postwar mode, Waugh's response was simply to amplify his role of haughty aristocrat.

Both writers were deeply suspicious of anything "in fashion," regardless of whether the prevailing winds blew in from the Right or from the Left. At the start of the cold war, when being pro-Russian suddenly became very unfashionable indeed, Waugh was as contemptuous of Senator Joseph McCarthy's witch hunting as he had been of Stalin's purges. In fact, when William F. Buckley, founder of the *National Review*, sent Waugh a copy of his book supporting Senator Joseph McCarthy and McCarthyism as a necessary evil, Waugh wrote back, "Your book makes plain that there was a need for investigation ten years ago. It does not, I am afraid, supply the information that would convince me that McCarthy was a suitable man to undertake it." Referring to a prominent journalistic critic of McCarthy, he added, "[Richard] Rovere makes a number of precise charges against his personal honor. Unless these are rebutted those who sympathize with his cause much deplore his championship of it." Waugh's is a high and admirable standard and on one occasion even Orwell failed to meet it, supplying to the British Foreign Office his list of names of suspected communist sympathizers. The names are either absurd or obvious, but the fact remains that he named them. If as principled a man as Orwell at least once could use bad means in a good fight, we can understand why so many opinion leaders did the same thing on a regular basis.

The antidote to all this nonsense would have to come from the average citizen. Both Orwell and Waugh believed that the common sense of the people was generally far superior to the theories of the best educated. Orwell, stunned at Germany's folly in invading Russia when Britain was unbeaten and America likely to come into the war, wrote, "So long as the common man can get a hearing, such elementary rules as not fighting all your enemies simultaneously are less likely to be violated." The elementary rules of common sense would probably have prevented an American land war in Asia and, years later, the precipitous effort to transplant democracy to sandy soil that had never sustained such roots.

Orwell and Waugh would have agreed that today "the elementary rules" of common sense are virtually ignored by political and opinion leaders. The urgent issues in most people's lives are peripheral to the concerns of our decision makers. In the United States the political system has been so perverted to inflate new class influence that both political parties have become controlled by extremists. The average American sees shouting heads on television and has little interest in or connection to whatever they're fighting about. Elections are won or lost by a few fervent factions in a few swing states. The consent of the governed has become in many ways a hollow phrase.

The Modern Age has seen the growing displacement of majority rule by the rulings of experts. Both the Tory Waugh and the socialist Orwell were united in their loathing of expertise. One of Waugh's great comic inventions is the character Basil Seal, superficially bright and impressively educated, but something of a con man who thinks himself an expert on everything. Seal is heavily based on Peter Rodd, who was married to Waugh's close friend Nancy Mitford. Before their marriage, Rodd spent a week at her home, "talking until the family reeled with boredom. No matter what subject was brought up, including the history of the tollgate system in the eighteenth and guage; he wrote with purity because he owed it to himself and to God to do his best at what he did best.

Orwell's output was primarily in essays and reviews. The short novels for which he is best known, *Animal Farm* and *1984*, were both illustrations of everything he'd said in his essays— all the things; a lifetime of insight on everything from language to class warfare is embodied in the people and events of his engrossing novels. He had written repeatedly that the best language is not abstract but linked to real things, to real life. He tried always to follow a general proposition with a specific example or a metaphor. He ended his life with two stories that made real for the reader virtually every idea he had ever expressed in the past.

Waugh, on the other hand, wrote primarily fiction, and much of it hilarious. In this regard he was in a sense closer to Orwell's precepts than even Orwell, who once wrote, "Every joke is a small revolution." Look at Orwell's "Politics and the English Language" and its observation that words can smother meaning as easily as they can clarify it. Waugh doesn't tell us this, he shows us. And we laugh.

We see this in Waugh's novel *Scoop*, perhaps the funniest debunking of journalism ever. In a few deft lines Waugh captures the obsequiousness of employee (Mr. Salter) to boss (the publisher Lord Copper):

> Mr. Salter's side of the conversation was limited to expressions of assent. When Lord Copper was right he said, "Definitely, Lord Copper"; when he was wrong "Up to a point."
>
> "Let me see, what's the name of the place I mean? Capital of Japan? Yokohama, isn't it?"

nineteenth centuries, it seemed he was the world expert. 'I know, I know,' he would interrupt. 'I know, I *was* an engineer and I . . .' or 'I know, I know, I *am* a farmer . . .' The sisters swore he once said, 'I know, I know, I *am* the Pope.' "

Waugh imagined what would happen if this overeducated fool was ever put in charge of a country. In his wonderful *Black Mischief* (1932), Basil Seal goes off to the African nation of Azania (the book was inspired by Waugh's attending the coronation of Haile Selassie). Seal is delighted to be in Azania. "Every year or so there's *one* place on the globe worth going to where things are happening. The secret is to find out where and be on the spot in time." On arrival he is recognized by the young emperor, Seth, who had met him once at Oxford where "Basil had enjoyed a reputation of peculiar brilliance among his contemporaries. . . . He had traveled all over Europe, spoke six languages, called dons by their Christian names and discussed their books with them." So Seth quickly makes Seal the high commissioner of the Ministry of Modernization, whose function is "to promote the adoption of modern organization and habits of life throughout the Azanian Empire." There is probably no better, and certainly no funnier, case to be made against nation building than what Waugh next has happen to Azania. A nation slowly evolving in compliance with its own customs and traditions is thrust cold turkey into the Modern Age, until the populace revolts (right in the middle of the Pageant of Birth Control), civil war ensues, the emperor is murdered, the heroine eaten, and the country deprived of independence, becoming a joint protectorate of England and France. Seal returns to England, looking for the next "one place on the globe" to be.

Orwell's hatred of the new class of rulers is even greater than Waugh's. His novel *1984* is, among other things, a searing indictment of the test-score meritocracy. The world is divided into three classes—the Inner Party, the Outer Party, and the Proles. Allocation to one class or another is determined by the scores of tests everyone takes at age sixteen. The most dystopian book ever written, the harshest portrayal of dictatorial evil, is about a society that is stratified by IQ. It isn't just Big Brother who tortures people and kills freedom. In fact, we're not even sure that there *is* a Big Brother. The villain we see is O'Brien, a member of the Inner Party. The Inner Party is composed of the people with the highest test scores. It is, as Orwell wrote elsewhere, "a hierarchical society where the intellectual can at last get his hands on the whip."

O'Brien personally supervises the appalling torture of Winston Smith, the central character of the book, an Outer Party member struggling against the assaults on his humanity. Smith knows, and O'Brien knows that he knows, that O'Brien is much smarter than he is. So how can he be right and O'Brien wrong? How can Smith be sure that torture and bullying and privation are bad and that freedom and decency are good? Because deep down he has an instinct of what the world should be. His instinct tells him that the harsh, austere, and enslaved world of his torturers is not inevitable. It is wrong. He can't prove this by a syllogism, but he *knows* it is wrong.

This is the quintessence of what Orwell and Waugh both feared most about modernity—"the perversion of instinct that has been made possible by the machine age," as Orwell wrote in an essay on Dali. He also wrote approvingly that the English people "will always prefer instinct to logic, and character to intelligence." These were Waugh's standards, too. He saw instinct and character as best exemplified by the aristocracy (despite his lampooning of them in *Vile Bodies*). But if the aristocrats died off or lapsed into degeneracy, then the upholders of instinct and character and common sense and decency would be what some intellectuals derisively called "the common man." The greatest threat to the virtues practiced by the average person would come from intellectuals themselves, if those intellectuals ever composed a class of their own. "Orthodoxies, whether of the Right or the Left, flourish chiefly among the literary intelligentsia, the people who ought in theory to be guardians of freedom of thought," Orwell noted.

Another highly distinctive feature of the Modern Age that both authors clearly foresaw was the retreat from religious faith. Orwell, the atheist, was at least as concerned as Waugh, the devout Catholic, about what this meant. He worried, time and again, in essays and articles, with increasing urgency, how people would live after ceasing to believe in immortality. He saw that a critical break from all of history was the loss of belief in life after death.

His concern with this change was largely political. He saw that when people believed in heaven and hell, they behaved differently than when they thought this life all that there was. He acknowledged that even in the centuries when religion was a dominant force, many people behaved in a way that would surely consign them to Hades on Judgment Day. His point was that they would have behaved far worse if they had not feared those flames. More important, many people had done acts of public good to tip the scales away from their private mischief. It was good for society that many feared eternal retribution for misspent lives. In the Modern Age, disbelief in an afterlife leaves nothing to live for but fun. Eat, drink, and be merry. You only get to go around once. This is exactly the mind-set that Waugh portrayed through the pointless, frenzied partying of

Vile Bodies. He wrote, as we have seen, that ten years of such hedonism had led to his conversion to Catholicism.

Now, Orwell did not believe in life after death, and Waugh was absolutely certain that it existed. In fact, when Orwell wrote that "few people now believe in life after death," Waugh harrumphed back in an essay of his own that everyone *he* knew believed in it. But this wasn't really true—surely not at all those parties that he couldn't stop attending. And the flight from faith has only intensified in our own time. It's clear that life today is highly hedonistic; an enormous amount of most people's time is spent not in the pursuit of happiness, but of fun—which is not at all the same thing. Yes, there's been a huge growth of fundamentalist religion in recent years, but that's merely a reaction to the steady loss of faith so evident elsewhere in our society. The mainstream churches are losing members and often seem devoted to causes more worthy than holy. No one can fail to see the coarsening of our general culture, and the new low standards are hardly compatible with a belief in higher powers.

Orwell scoffed at "religious reactionaries—that is, people who defend an unjust order of society by claiming that the world cannot be substantially improved and only the 'next world' matters." He might have been speaking of Waugh. "One must choose between this world and the next," he concluded.

That was the political Orwell speaking. But the great thing about him was his stubborn insistence on objective truth, even when it meant admitting he had made a mistake. He was like someone from another planet dropped to earth and describing what he saw with neither preconception nor the slightest regard to local reaction. He therefore could see that people who no longer believed in an afterlife were more likely to become triathletes than reformers. This troubled him. He wanted the moral imperative of religion without having religion itself. But he came to see how hard this was to achieve. He saw that part of the appeal of the dictatorships he opposed was their pomp and ceremony and leader worship that filled the void where faith had been. He saw the need for something *like* religion—his vision of a socialist Britain actually included retention of the monarch, because he recognized that people had a need for belief in something beyond themselves. Orwell believed that part of the attraction of Hitler to the Germans was his reliance on pageantry and uniforms and stirring music, all of which provided a substitute for weakened religion.

It is amazing, given his atheism, how close this brought him to Waugh's views on the same subject. Waugh agreed entirely with Orwell's statement that one must choose between this world and the next. But for him the clear choice was the next world. He found it absurd to think that social progress could be made in a moral void, or that a moral code could exist without religion. In 1930, just after converting to Catholicism, Waugh was handsomely paid for an article in the *Daily Express* explaining why he had done so. He wrote:

> It was nearly two centuries before the real nature of [the] loss of faith became apparent.
>
> Today we can see it on all sides as the active negation of all that western culture has stood for. Civilization—and by this I do not mean talking cinemas and tinned food, nor even surgery and hygienic houses, but the whole moral and artistic organization of Europe—has not in itself the power of survival. It came into being through Christianity, and without it has no significance or power

to command allegiance. The loss of faith in Christianity and the consequential loss of confidence in moral and social standards have become embodied in the ideal of a materialistic, mechanized state, already existent in Russia and rapidly spreading south and west. It is no longer possible, as it was in the time of Gibbon, to accept the benefits of civilization and at the same time deny the supernatural basis on which it rests. As the issues become clearer the polite skeptic and with him that purely fictitious figure, the happy hedonist, will disappear.

Both men, then, came by different routes to the view that the Modern Age would be faithless, and consequently something essential would be missing from our lives, displaced but not replaced by hedonism.

There was a backlash to the loss of faith. Vast numbers of Americans in recent years reported that their votes were swayed more by moral values than by any other concern. This is often mistakenly seen as suggesting that one party is more moral than another. But that was never true. It means instead that people of all political views have grasped that moral certitude is gone from their society, and this realization troubles them.

No, neither Orwell nor Waugh saw in the Modern Age the steady upward progress so comforting to H. G. Wells. They saw instead a bottomless abyss, which one man believed could be escaped in the next world, and the other resolutely sought to bridge by a moral code in this life.

THERE IS ONE MORE THING that both saw coming, and no other portent could so terribly chill their hearts: the assault on language. All language of course, but they cared specifically about the English language, which no one wrote better in the twentieth century, or ever.

And the perversion of the English language that alarmed them in their own time has in ours exceeded even their worst fears.

If George Orwell had never written *1984*, or *Animal Farm*, or indeed anything else but his single essay "Politics and the English Language," then his name still would be revered today. A small but fervent audience would cherish it and the best teachers assign it; friends would share it with one another, as is the case right now.

The essay is a warning about how language controls thought. It is evident that people who don't think clearly can't speak clearly, but Orwell pointed out that the reverse is true as well. If we are not accustomed or trained to speak precisely then our ideas will be imprecise, too. Language should be rooted in reality.

This is serious stuff. We are—and we do—what we think, and we can only think fully in language. As an example Orwell said if we are trained to say "pacification" rather than "killing the people in a village" our actions, and the reaction to our actions, will be different. He pointed out a great many other problems, as well, such as the vagueness of speech by politicians, in which an endless spoken paragraph can convey no idea or position at all.

Orwell's link of language and thought informs a large part of *1984*, from the steadily shrinking Newspeak to the Ministry of Love where people are tortured.

Waugh was greatly concerned with language, too. But he wasn't out to make the world a better place through better lan-

"Up to a point, Lord Copper."

"And Hong Kong belongs to us, doesn't it?"

"Definitely, Lord Copper."

Whether as a cause or a joke, language mattered more to Orwell and Waugh than did anything else. And so today's world would have driven them mad.

For one thing, they understood that communication was not a solitary exercise. You had to communicate *with* someone else. They both came out the same way on that much-debated tree falling in the forest: Someone had to *hear* it fall. Both men wrote for readers. There was none of this I-write-for-myself nonsense. Waugh entertained a relatively small and sophisticated audience, though it made him famous and comfortable in his lifetime. Throughout most of his life, Orwell had a smaller (though steadily growing) readership, but when it came to summing up his work through fiction he thought globally. One of the reasons *Animal Farm* is a simply written short parable is so that it could be translated easily into foreign languages and enjoyed even by those of limited education. He wanted to reach people living under totalitarian rule, and he certainly did. It was the same with *1984*. People under Soviet rule were amazed that a citizen of a free country had so fully understood the kind of existence they had to endure. (His experiences in Spain helped inform him, as did dealing with the London literary establishment.)

What Orwell and Waugh would have found infuriating about our time is that many writers today do not want a diverse audience. They write only for people exactly like themselves. We have seen that our society is as stratified as was England in the 1930s, though in different ways. The caste of the best educated communicates far too often in the abstract, lifeless, and maddeningly generalized prose against which Orwell so strongly inveighed. It's not that the average person cannot understand them but rather that no sensible person would want to.

An excellent example of speech so abstract that it's meaningless was given by a presidential candidate in an interview in which he tried to praise the French philosopher Maurice Merleau-Ponty's *Phenomenology of Perception,* a book, the politician explained, he found helpful "in cultivating a capacity for a more refined introspection that gave me better questions that ultimately led to a renewed determination to become involved with the effort to make things better." And the interviewer was favorably impressed by this appalling inflation of language! What the politician was actually trying to say, as best one can determine, is that a French writer made him think more clearly and therefore better able to do good. The sentence as delivered should really be inserted into Orwell's "Politics and the English Language"; it's a better illustration than even he could find.

It's hard to know why so many intelligent people choose to write and speak this way. Perhaps, in a phrase Waugh used in another context, they speak to inform rather than to attract. They are informing their highly educated peers of their shared class identity. They have no interest in attracting converts. Being accessible to the average reader is to some authors a source of shame.

This has very little to do with the traditional political concepts of Right and Left. The conservative writer William Buckley has from the start been respected, though not followed, by many educated people who do not agree with a word he has to say. This is due to the plumpness of his vocabulary and the complexity of his verbal constructions. The same point, to some extent, may be made about George F. Will. These two conservatives are read regularly, if disapprovingly, by people who would change the station at the first sound of Rush Limbaugh's voice, even when the message is much the same. It's a question of respecting one's own perceived class members, regardless of what they have to say.

Modern technology has greatly facilitated the segregation of audiences. Each group of listeners, viewers, or readers has its own language, even intonation: Just think of those National Public Radio voices whose atonality seems deliberate, as if through fear of favoring one syllable over another and thereby offending some perfectly dispassionate enforcer of equal opportunity for vowels. Presidential elections can be decided by the way a candidate speaks, and the class identity that implies. Orwell observed that, in a different era of class division, Churchill's great popularity with the general public was partly related to his lack of the patronizing upper-class accent.

And the rock bottom, the nadir, the living end (except that it isn't living) of speech today is its transformation by technology. Think e-mail. To put it mildly, many people no longer communicate in complete sentences. Speed is life. "You" is now "u" because it's quicker, and u are in big trouble if you don't know where that leads. Condensation of language can be good—as Waugh would say—up to a point. That point is where limited language becomes limited thought. An important idea in *1984* is that language under Big Brother is deliberately becoming smaller—there are fewer and fewer words; as the vocabulary of dissent shrivels so must dissent. The vocabulary of many of our best-educated people is now shrinking in their communication with their colleagues, words jettisoned not by a censor but by a BlackBerry.

We should recall that in the world of *1984* nothing written was permanent. It had to be thrown on order down the memory hole and burned. But not even Orwell imagined that people would erase their own words voluntarily, all the time, and just because they *could*. The impermanence of a written record permits a future not only independent from but ignorant of the past.

To the two greatest English writers of the last century, each of whom saw tradition as the banister and not the barrier to ascension, nothing would rival the delete button as the scariest feature of our own time.

And even apart from the debasement and impermanence of language, many of the most highly educated among us seem unable to discuss general ideas at all. The best and the brightest have become specialists. Their careers and status increasingly depend on a precise specificity within each professional niche. Their speech is vague and their knowledge constricted.

Some who still do have the will to seek broader knowledge no longer have the time. Uniquely in world history, the best educated and most affluent have the least leisure.

The golden twilight of the leisured classes ensured both contemplation and erudition. Out of immersion in the great wealth of past culture could come new thought to add to our heritage—but no longer, save on campuses for those faculty members brave enough to ignore the political correctness of their colleagues.

Orwell and Waugh were well educated in Latin and Greek, and the purity of their prose was the enduring result. They read omnivorously all their lives, not merely the vast treasury of English literature, but the best of the rest of the Western canon, too. While they worked hard, the work was chosen by them alone, the reading selected purely for itself, their own artful phrases and upsetting thoughts the product of leisure.

For real leisure is not laziness. It is in fact quite busy, and it permits a fullness of life denied to narrow specialists whose time passes in billable hours. Aristotle defined happiness as the full employment of one's faculties along lines of excellence. So grim Orwell and bored Waugh in fact led happy lives—the reason they were happy was that they were free.

There is supposedly so much more freedom in our world than in theirs. But perhaps even fewer lives are truly free. The time between birth and death is all too fleeting, and life is a train that picks up speed. To waste it is sinful.

It was in the freedom and courage to choose one's own life that Orwell and Waugh were most nearly the same. That their lives were deliberately chosen is the most valuable legacy that both offer to us now, in our own so-busy time.

Epilogue

—

ORWELL DIED ALONE. THE VISITORS, AND EVEN HIS NEW wife, had left the hospital in the early evening, hoping he would be able to get some sleep. Just after midnight on January 21, 1950, a blood vessel in his lung ruptured and he bled to death. Perhaps he tried to call for help, but no one heard.

In announcing his death to the world, the BBC broadcast a clock striking thirteen.

Orwell's funeral service took place at Christ Church in London. His will, written only a few days earlier, had requested a church funeral and that he be buried "according to the rights [*sic*] of the Church of England in the nearest convenient cemetery." This must have seemed to Orwell the traditional English thing to do. The cemetery chosen was that of All Saints Church, in Sutton Courtney, Berkshire—Orwell had not been a congregant of any church, so finding a cemetery was difficult, but David Astor owned the estate adjoining All Saints and was able one last time to use his influence on his friend's behalf. The simple headstone reads HERE LIES ERIC ARTHUR BLAIR. BORN JUNE 25TH, 1903. DIED JANUARY 21ST, 1950. Just behind it today is David Astor's grave.

"G. Orwell is dead and Mrs. Orwell presumably a rich widow," wrote Waugh to Nancy Mitford. "Mrs. Orwell" was the deathbed bride, Sonia Brownell, who legally was Mrs. Blair. But she called herself Sonia Orwell until her own death, in 1980.

It was reasonable for Waugh to presume she had become rich. Orwell left his entire estate to Sonia, with Richard to receive the remainder after her death, and, until then, an allowance. For thirty years Sonia was the beneficiary of the royalties of one of the bestselling writers of all time, yet there is no evidence that she received or spent vast sums. Many have asked, with no satisfactory answer, what ever happened to all that money? There was enough for Sonia to live in modest comfort and to accumulate some capital, and for Richard to receive his allowance. But the mystery of the missing millions remains.

Sonia took her role as keeper of George Orwell's flame very seriously and she did the job well. At his death, his worldwide fame was associated almost entirely with *Animal Farm* and *1984*, whose publication coincided with the advent of the cold war. Orwell would have been bemused by how respectable he had become. Right and Left continue to battle over the question of which side he really was closer to.

But there was more to Orwell than two famous books, and Sonia helped focus attention on the brilliant journalism and essays that had preceded them. Together with an able assistant, Ian Angus, in 1968 she published *The Collected Essays, Journalism and Letters of George Orwell*, a four-volume set that has assured Orwell's place in English literature as the finest essayist of our time.

And she did something else for Orwell, too. She ensured that Richard would receive his inheritance. She obviously had not looked out for her own money—she never seemed to press the accountants on why there was so little cash, and at their suggestion she even signed over the ownership of Orwell's copyrights to a legal entity over which she had no control. When she knew she was dying, she bought the copyrights back—for £250,000, all the money she had after thirty years of supposedly receiving royalties. She died without a cent. But Richard had his legacy; the royalties were then paid to him.

Richard Blair was raised by Avril Blair, Eric's sister, and her husband, Bill Dunn. They moved from Jura to the Scottish mainland. Richard studied at Lackham College of Agriculture in Wiltshire. He did postgraduate work at the North of Scotland Agricultural College, in Aberdeen. He took up farming, and then worked as an agricultural engineer. In 1964, he married Eleanor Mair. They have two sons, Gavin and Alastar, and Eleanor is now a magistrate. And somewhere up there, if Waugh was right about heaven, George Orwell is taking time out from critiquing the angels, and gazing happily at his grandsons.

EVELYN WAUGH LIVED sixteen years longer than George Orwell. By the time of Orwell's death he, too, had reached the most successful point of his career. *Brideshead Revisited* had moved him from being the toast of a set to far wider fame. He was held in the highest critical esteem as well.

None of this seemed to bring him much money. Waugh's financial disappointments may help explain why the widow Orwell wasn't able to bank more cash, either. The problem, in a word, was taxation. British taxation. The costs of the war would have required any government to raise taxes, and the Attlee government placed as much of the burden as possible on the rich. The tax on earned income over £5,000 was so high that many thought it pointless to earn more. Over the years, Waugh's writing had brought him a comfortable income, but no more than that. With *Brideshead Revisited* he finally hit pay dirt, but the Inland Revenue kept him from keeping it.

Waugh found himself destitute. He had a large accumulation of dollars in America, and he went there several times in order to be able to spend it. (He would have had even more, but MGM wanted Charles to end up with Julia after all and so he didn't let his bestseller be filmed.) He did his best to avoid the confiscatory tax, but he still had six children to educate, and most of the servants at Piers Court had to be let go.

Even so, the sort of people who had found Orwell insufficiently Marxist now criticized Waugh for living like a lord. The new class foreseen and loathed by both writers was increasingly in charge of things, particularly public opinion, and saw Waugh as a country squire absorbed with status and concealing his own roots. He was interviewed by the BBC in 1953, and the program was a perfect demonstration of meritless members of the meritocracy attacking a writer far beyond their own gifts because they deemed him politically incorrect. Waugh remained serene throughout their assault. When asked his opinion of "the man on the street," he said, "I have never encountered such a person." He added, "There are individual men and women, each one of whom has an individual and immortal soul, and such beings need to use the street from time to time." When the interviewer, disdainful of Waugh's support of capital punishment, asked if Waugh would have been willing personally to serve as hangman, Waugh calmly replied that it seemed unlikely that the government would choose a novelist to perform such a task.

Waugh was weak and he was exhausted—from writing everything he could in order to support his family, from the sleeplessness that his work provoked, and above all from the drugs he then took in order to sleep—in far greater doses than was safe, even if he hadn't habitually mixed them with crème de menthe. He was poisoning himself and finally went mad, beset by invisible tormentors. With the support of his family and through his own iron will he was eventually able to stop taking the damaging drugs.

He lived until 1966. He wrote other books and many articles, and in the 1950s he produced a trilogy about the Second World War that was published in England under the title *Sword of Honour*. These short novels (*Men at Arms, Officers and Gentlemen,* and *Unconditional Surrender*) are fictional accounts of his own service, but each soldier's war is the whole war, and, just as he had served his nation with honor though physically past his prime, so did his prose regain its strength and subtlety when he set out to chronicle England's finest hour, which in the writing became his own as well. Many regard *Sword of Honour* as his best work. It sums up the war as a fight to preserve common decency, and it is clear he believed the struggle had been lost.

In 1956 the Waugh family moved from Piers Court to another grand house, Combe Florey, in Somerset. Waugh was famous and his status as a writer secure, but the personal attacks on his aristocratic lifestyle and unfashionable views were an ongoing irritant. For a man who had found the Modern Age untenable even in the 1920s, one can imagine his disgust with the 1960s. The Age of Aquarius was not for him; he preferred Aquinas.

His last years were not happy. He suffered from depression, obesity, bad hearing, and bad temper. He coveted a knighthood, but it never was offered, and he declined a lesser honor. A far greater disappointment was caused by the reforms in the Catholic Church instituted by Pope John XXIII. The use of English in the mass symbolized for him retreat from a tradition that was the bedrock of faith.

Evelyn Waugh died on Easter Sunday in 1966, suddenly, at home, of a coronary thrombosis. He was sixty-three, but for some time had seemed much older.

His Requiem Mass at Westminster Cathedral was conducted in Latin, as Waugh had requested. He was buried near Combe Florey, and the headstone reads simply, "Evelyn Waugh. Writer."

His wife, Laura, lived on at Combe Florey until her death in 1973. His son Bron's widow, Lady Teresa Waugh, lives there today.

Whether or not he was a noble descendant, Waugh was unquestionably a first-class ancestor. He seems to have founded a literary dynasty. A number of his children proved themselves to be fine writers. Bron wrote several novels and was an exceptionally popular and controversial columnist. Bron's son Alexander is a wise and witty writer, as evidenced by his book *Fathers and Sons*, which deals hilariously with the filial relations of all the Waughs from the Brute to his own small son, Bron. Some of Alexander's siblings, as well as his mother, are also accomplished writers.

EVELYN WAUGH ROWED AGAINST the tide as steadfastly as did George Orwell, and in their wake is our path.

ACKNOWLEDGMENTS

After I had been working on this book for about a year, my wife remarked that Orwell and Waugh seemed to have moved into our home. She was right, so let me first acknowledge, in a contemporary phrase, the three people in my marriage while this work progressed.

First, there is my wife, Randy Miller Lebedoff, who preceded the two intruders and patiently put up with them until they were gone, but was always first, even in that company, and in every other way. I acknowledge gratefully that she is my life.

And gratitude is due as well to our long-term tenants, George Orwell and Evelyn Waugh. I started reading Waugh in my teens, and Orwell soon after, but in his case just the two short books whose names are known to all. And then, almost forty years ago, a kind friend gave me the four volumes, then just published, of Orwell's essays and other nonfiction. I was dazzled then and still am today on opening one of those sturdy tomes to any page. I put them in a place of honor on a shelf beside the fireplace. They are the most finely crafted works written in the twentieth century—in nonfiction, that is, for the shelves on the other side of our fireplace hold Waugh's novels, those little tattered paperbacks perhaps even more perfectly wrought than the stern hard-covered volumes of Orwell's work, and always, however often read, miraculously, howlingly funny.

And through the years, it did not matter from which side of the fireplace I picked one favorite over another; in either case, I always found—as Waugh wrote of an aging burgundy—that my chance selection "still spoke in the pure, authentic accent of its prime and . . . in the same lapidary phrase, the same words of hope."

In time I came to see how similar were the writers of such unfailing joys, and how far our own world was moving from what those two men held most vital.

To call them the same man is to invite dissent because, of course, the way they lived seems perfectly contrasted. But what they lived for was not. And we all need to know what that was.

THERE ARE MANY PEOPLE to whom I'm grateful for assistance in this project. My children, Caroline, Jonathan, and Nick, accepted with alacrity and ill-concealed relief my request to leave their father to his labors. My brother and sisters, Jonathan Lebedoff, Judy Lebedoff, and Lisa Peilen, served as mine-sweepers for the first drafts, as did my friends Harry Walsh, Phil Shively, Diane Lilly, Tom and Victoria Johnson, Bill Dolan, Beth Dooley, Chris Malstead, Bill Griswold, Brian Palmer, Jim Tucker, Bill Pohlad, Paul Rexford Thatcher, Greg Wierzynski, Loren and Frances Rothschild, Ryan Winkler, Jack El Hai, Dennis Haley, and Bob and Margee Kinney.

Then there are the English, who assisted us so greatly. The staff of the Orwell Archive at University College, London, were exceptionally hospitable and helpful as my wife and I foraged greedily among their papers.

The Waugh family could not have been more gracious and sharing. Alexander Waugh, Evelyn's grandson and himself a fine writer, presides over a charming home in Somerset that contains two glowing treasures: his own lovely family, and the mother lode of Waviana, an astonishing collection of letters, diaries, photographs, notes, clippings, articles, books, and other memorabilia of Evelyn Waugh and the rest of his literary clan. Alexander transformed his music room into a working library for our visit, a huge table somehow sustaining the weight of a full platoon of boxes uniformly clad in soft green leather, each containing its packed share of precious paper. We shall always be grateful to Alexander and Eliza Waugh for the warmth of their hospitality. And I have no happier memory than that of my wife's peals of laughter as she read from the original copies of Evelyn Waugh's unsurpassable correspondence.

Alexander's mother, Lady Teresa Waugh, the widow of Evelyn's son Auberon, was kind enough to let us visit her at Combe Florey, the family home. And Evelyn's firstborn, Teresa Waugh D'Arms, graciously welcomed me into her home in Ann Arbor, Michigan, and shared her rich memories and heritage.

I thank Random House for taking on this project, and Susanna Porter, my editor, whose skill and diligence were enormously helpful to me and to this book. Jillian Quint gets a medal for patience, good humor, and tireless professionalism. Michelle Daniel raised copyediting to an art form, her every scrawl a mark of keen intelligence. Production editor Janet Wygal is a saint.

Thanks and blessings to my agent, Jonathon Lazear, bigger than life but far more comforting, and to Christi Cardenas of the Lazear Agency, who is always patient, sunny, and wise.

APPENDIX I

Chronology

—

ORWELL	WAUGH
JUNE 25, 1903: Eric Arthur Blair is born in Motihari, Bengal, India.	OCTOBER 28, 1903: Evelyn Arthur St. John Waugh is born at 11 Hillfield Road, Hampstead.
1904: Blair is brought to England, to the family home at Henley-on-Thames.	
1907: Richard Blair (Eric's father) returns for three months' leave, then goes back to India until 1912.	1907: Waugh family moves to North End Road, Hampstead.
1908–1911: Attends Anglican day school in Henley-on-Thames.	1910–1917: Attends Heath Mount, a local day school.
1911–1916: Attends St. Cyprian's preparatory school, in Sussex.	
1917–1921: Attends Eton College as King's Scholar. Blairs move to Southwold.	1917–1921: Attends Lancing College preparatory school, in Sussex.
1922–1927: Works as assistant superintendent of police, Indian Imperial Police, Burma.	1922–1924: Attends Hertford College, Oxford.
	1925–1927: Works as schoolmaster in Wales, then in Berkshire, then in London. Becomes journalist for *Daily Express*.
1928–1929: Lives in Paris. Works as dishwasher and is hospitalized with pneumonia.	1928–1929: Publishes first book, *Rossetti: His Life and Works*. Marries Evelyn Gardner. Publishes *Decline and Fall*.

ORWELL	WAUGH
1930–1931: Goes tramping through English countryside; picks hops in Kent; starts to write.	1930-1931: Divorces Evelyn Gardner. Publishes *Vile Bodies*, bestseller. Becomes Roman Catholic. Travels to Abyssinia.
1932–1933: Teaches school.	1932: Publishes *Black Mischief*. Travels widely throughout the world.
1933–1934: Assumes the pen name George Orwell. Publishes first book, *Down and Out in Paris and London*. Moves to Hampstead.	1933–1934: Publishes travel books and *A Handful of Dust*.
1935: Publishes *A Clergyman's Daughter;* meets Eileen O'Shaughnessy.	1935: Publishes *Edmund Campion*. Works as war journalist in Abyssinia and Italy. Travels.
1936: Lives among unemployed workers. Publishes *Keep the Aspidistra Flying*. Marries Eileen O'Shaughnessy.	1936: Marriage is annulled. Abyssinia again. Writes travel accounts, short stories.
1937: Fights in Spanish Civil War, wounded. *The Road to Wigan Pier* is published.	1937: Marries Laura Herbert. Moves into Piers Court.
1938: *Homage to Catalonia* is published. Spends six months in tuberculosis sanatorium.	1938: Teresa is born. *Scoop* is published. Waugh travels to Hungary and Mexico.
SEPTEMBER 3, 1939: WAR DECLARED	
1939: *Coming Up for Air* is published, essays and articles.	1939: Auberon is born. Waugh joins Royal Marines.
1940–1943: Joins Home Guard. Reviews for several publications. Publishes essays and articles. Works as producer and broadcaster, BBC.	1940–1943: Serves in Dakar, Crete, and Scotland. Publishes *Put Out More Flags*. Mary born; dies. Margaret is born.

ORWELL	WAUGH
1944: Eric and Eileen adopt Richard. Finishes *Animal Farm*.	1944: In Yugoslavia with Randolph Churchill. Harriet is born.
AUGUST 15, 1945: WAR ENDS	
1945: Eileen dies. *Animal Farm* is published.	1945: *Brideshead Revisited* is published.
1946–1948: Lives in Jura with Richard. Writes much of *1984*. Health worsens.	1946–1948: Travels extensively outside England, including United States. James is born. *The Loved One* is published.
1949: Health worsens. Enters Cranham Sanatorium. *1984* is published to enormous success. Enters London hospital. Marries Sonia Brownell.	1949: Returns from United States. Lives as country squire.
1950: Dies on January 21 in London hospital.	1950–1954: Continues world travels. Publishes *Helena*. Septimus is born. *Men at Arms* is published. First novel of World War II trilogy is published. Suffers temporary insanity caused by medication and alcohol.
	1955: Publishes second volume of trilogy, *Officers and Gentlemen*.
	1956: Moves to Combe Florey House.
	1957: Publishes novel on his breakdown, *The Ordeal of Gilbert Pinfold*.

ORWELL	WAUGH
	1958–1963: Bron is wounded in Cyprus. Waugh publishes *Ronald Knox* and final novel of trilogy, *Unconditional Surrender*. (In the United States, titled *The End of the Battle*.)
	1964: Publishes first volume of autobiography, *A Little Learning*.
	1966: Publishes trilogy in revised volume, titled *Sword of Honour*. Dies on April 10, Easter Sunday, at Combe Florey.

APPENDIX II

Orwell's Reading List for 1949

[FROM *THE COMPLETE WORKS OF GEORGE ORWELL*
(TWENTY VOLUMES), APPENDIX 4]

In the last year of his life, Orwell's declining health kept him from writing. But he could still read. An appendix to *The Complete Works of George Orwell*, edited by Peter Davison, prints the list that Orwell had made of the books he read in 1949. It is an amazing list, not only in depth and variety, but as an indication, if one were needed, that the writer who consistently valued the wisdom of the people far more highly than the pronouncements of intellectuals, exemplified in his own life the highest standards of intellectual dispassion and rigor. (The asterisks and question marks appear in Orwell's original manuscript.)

January

AUTHOR	TITLE	REMARKS
F. SCOTT FITZGERALD	*Tender Is the Night*	
*D. H. LAWRENCE	*Sons & Lovers*	
E. ARNOT ROBINSON	*Four Frightened People*	
J. L. & B. HAMMOND	*The Town Labourer*	Skimmed only
T. S. ELIOT	*From Poe to Valéry*	
BARRY PAIN	*The Eliza Books*	
*ARNOLD BENNETT	*Riceyman Steps*	
*V. SACKVILLE WEST	*The Edwardians*	
*E. A. POE	*Tales*	Most of them
E. C. WEBSTER	*Ceremony of Innocence*	
BERTRAND RUSSELL	*Human Knowledge, Its Scope and Limits*	Tried and failed
PETER CHEYNEY	*Dark Hero*	
HAROLD NICHOLSON	*Public Faces*	
JAMES CAIN	*The Postman Always Rings Twice*	

February

AUTHOR	TITLE	REMARKS
THOMAS HARDY	*Jude the Obscure*	
JULIAN SYMONS	*Bland Beginning*	
*D. H. LAWRENCE	*The Prussian Officer*	
MARKOOSHA FISCHER	*The Nazarovs*	Skimmed only
ALDOUS HUXLEY	*Ape & Essence*	
*W. BARBELLION	*The Journal of a Disappointed Man*	
?R. CARGOE	*The Tormentors*	Proof copy
P. GOSSE	*A Naturalist Goes to War*	
*J. D. BERESFORD	*A Candidate for Truth*	
M. ALDANOV	*The Ninth Thermidor*	
*THOMAS HARDY	*Tess o'the D'Urbervilles*	
EVELYN WAUGH	*Robbery Under Law*	
EVELYN WAUGH	*When the Going Was Good*	
TANYA MATTHEWS	*Russian Child & Russian Wife*	Skimmed only
EVELYN WAUGH	*Rossetti: His Life & Works*	

March

AUTHOR	TITLE	REMARKS
?M. McCARTHY	*The Oasis* (in *Horizon*)	
*HESKETH PEARSON	*Dickens, His Character, Comedy & Career* (in proof)	
PHILIP GIBBS	*Both Your Houses*	
DELISLE BURNS	*The First Europe*	Skimmed
"SAKI"	*The Chronicles of Clovis*	
*I. ZANGWILL	*Children of the Ghetto*	
JAMES THURBER	*The Beast in Me*	
JOSEPH CONRAD	*Notes on Life & Letters*	

AUTHOR	TITLE	REMARKS
G. FAIRLEY	*Captain Bulldog Drummond*	
*J. FRAZER	*Folk Lore in the O.T.*	Dipped into
WINSTON CHURCHILL	*Their Finest Hour*	
EVELYN WAUGH	*Work Suspended*	
G. BERNARD SHAW	*Sixteen Autobiographical Sketches*	
	April	
*CHARLES DICKENS	*Little Dorrit*	
C. A. ALINGTON	*Archdeacons Afloat*	
M. BUBER-NEUMANN	*Under Two Dictators*	
M. BLOCH	*Strange Defeat*	
R. FISCHER	*Stalin & German Communism*	
?HANS SCHERFIG	*The Idealists*	
SIDNEY HORLER	*High Hazard*	
PETER CHEYNEY	*Try Anything Twice*	
R. SURTEES	*Mr. Sponge's Sporting Tour*	
	May	
*HUGH KINGSMILL	*The Sentimental Journey*	
GEOFFREY GORER	*The Americans*	
*GEORGE GISSING	*New Grub Street*	
F. TENNYSON JESSE	*A Pin to See the Peepshow*	
W. WHITE	*A Man Called White*	Skimmed
R. T. GOULD	*The Story of the Typewriter* (pamphlet)	
S. LABIN	*Stalin's Russia*	Skimmed only
*M. SINCLAIR	*The Combined Maze*	
*ARNOLD BENNETT	*Clayhanger*	

May (cont'd)

AUTHOR	TITLE	REMARKS
EDMUND WILSON	*The Triple Thinkers*	
D. SHUB	*Lenin*	Skimmed
ANTHONY POWELL	*John Aubrey & His Friends*	
LANCELOT HOGBEN	*The New Authoritarianism* (pamphlet)	
C. D. DARLINGTON	*The Conflict of Science and Society* (pamphlet)	
HENRY GREEN	*Loving*	
PATRICK HASTINGS	*Autobiography*	
C. BROOKS	*Modern Poetry & the Tradition*	Skimmed
HENRY GREEN	*Concluding*	
J. M. KEYNES	*Two Memoirs*	
OSBERT SITWELL	*Laughter in the Next Room*	
REX WARNER	*Why Was I Killed?*	

June

AUTHOR	TITLE	REMARKS
J. GUEST	*Broken Images*	
B. COBB	*Early Morning Poison*	
GEOFFREY TREASE	*Tales Out of School*	
G. SANTAYANA	*The Genteel Tradition at Bay* (pamphlet)	
WILLIAM EMPSON	*Seven Types of Ambiguity*	
J. J. FARJEON	*Seven Dead*	
*CYRIL CONNOLLY	*Enemies of Promise*	
N. WEST	*Miss Lonelyhearts*	
?A. WILSON	*The Wrong Set*	
J. GLOAG	*Documents Marked Secret*	
G. M. TREVELYAN	*An Autobiography & Other Essays*	Skimmed

AUTHOR	TITLE	REMARKS
I. DEUTSCHER	*Stalin: A Political Biography*	
*E. RAYMOND	*We, the Accused*	
*ARNOLD BENNETT	*Whom God Hath Joined*	
?WILLIAM SANSOM	*The Body*	
July		
W. SOMERSET MAUGHAM	*The Razor's Edge*	
*RUDYARD KIPLING	*The Day's Work*	
H. G. WELLS	*The Autocracy of Mr. Parham*	
PHILIP GUEDELLA	*The Duke*	
W. SOMERSET MAUGHAM	*Then & Now*	
J. M. KEYNES	*The Economic Consequences of the Peace*	Skimmed
?*T. DREISER	*Chains*	Skimmed
NEVIL SHUTE	*No Highway*	
GEORGE WOODCOCK	*The Paradox of Oscar Wilde*	
*T. DREISER	*Sister Carrie*	
E. SACKVILLE WEST	*A Flame in Sunlight*	Skimmed
*T. DREISER	*An American Tragedy*	
J. CURTIS	*The Gilt Kid*	
August		
J. COUSINS	*Secret Valleys*	
M. JOSEPH	*The Adventure of Publishing*	

August (cont'd)

AUTHOR	TITLE	REMARKS
DOROTHY SAYERS	*Mystery Omnibus*	Most of
H. M. HYDE	*Trials of Oscar Wilde*	Most of
NIGEL BALCHIN	*The Small Back Room*	
*NORMAN MAILER	*The Naked & the Dead*	[large asterisk]
M. DAVIDSON	*Astronomy for Beginners*	Skimmed
PHILIP GUEDELLA	*The Hundred Days*	
RAYMOND CHANDLER	*The Little Lady*	
A. BERKELEY	*Murder in the House*	
F.M. MONTGOMERY[1]	*Normandy to the Baltic*	Dipped into
J. LANGDON-DAVIES	*Russian Puts the Clock Back*	
*COMPTON MACKENZIE	*Sinister Street*	
AGATHA CHRISTIE	*Sparkling Cyanide*	

September

AUTHOR	TITLE	REMARKS
ARTHUR KOESTLER	*Promise and Fulfillment*	
J. M. BURNS	*The Gallery*	Most of
PHILIP TOYNBEE	*The Savage Days*	
W. H. SHELDON	*The Varieties of Temperament*	Skimmed
C. SYKES	*Character & Situation*	
R. WEST	*The Meaning of Treason*	
TRUMAN CAPOTE	*Other Voices, Other Rooms*	
F. UTLEY	*Lost Illusion*	
R. STOUT	*How Like a God*	
NANCY MITFORD	*Love in a Cold Climate*	
JULIAN SYMONS	*A. J. Symons* (in proof)	

[[1] "F.M." stands here for field marshal; Montgomery's initials were B.L.]

October

AUTHOR	TITLE	REMARKS
F. URQUHART	*The Year of the Short Corn*	
? ALBERTO MORAVIA	*The Woman of Rome*	
C. SYKES	*Four Studies in Loyalty*	
D. FOOTMAN	*Red Prelude*	
LEONARD WOOLLEY	*Digging Up the Past*	
L.A.S. SALAZAR	*Murder in Mexico* (proof)	Skimmed
RAYNER HEPPENSTALL	*The Double Image*	

November

AUTHOR	TITLE	REMARKS
OSCAR WILDE	*De Profundis* (new edition)	
*R. KEE	*The Impossible Shore*	
T. HOPKINSON	*Down the Long Slide*	
R. KEE	*A Crowd Is Not Compulsory*	
A. MENEN	*The Stumbling-Stone*	

December

AUTHOR	TITLE	REMARKS
E. H. CARR	*The Romantic Exiles*	
*JOSEPH CONRAD	*Chance*	
*JOSEPH CONRAD	*The Secret Agent*	
*JOSEPH CONRAD	*Under Western Eyes*	
*JOSEPH CONRAD	*The Nigger of the Narcissus*	
JULIAN HUXLEY	*Soviet Genetics*[2]	
MALCOLM MUGGERIDGE	*Affairs of the Heart*	

144 books, of which 27 read before, and 3 or 4 merely pamphlets.

[2 See p. 3725, n. 13., of *The Complete Works of George Orwell*.]

WORKS

—

BY GEORGE ORWELL

Down and Out in Paris and London, 1933
Burmese Days, 1934
A Clergyman's Daughter, 1935
Keep the Aspidistra Flying, 1936
The Road to Wigan Pier, 1937
Homage to Catalonia, 1938
Coming Up for Air, 1939
Inside the Whale, 1940
The Lion and the Unicorn, 1941
Animal Farm, 1945
1984, 1949

The Complete Works of George Orwell (twenty volumes), edited by Peter Davison, assisted by Ian Angus and Sheila Davison, 1998.

The Collected Essays, Journalism and Letters of George Orwell (four volumes), edited by Sonia Orwell and Ian Angus, 1968.

BY EVELYN WAUGH

FICTION

Decline and Fall, 1928

Vile Bodies, 1930

Black Mischief, 1932

A Handful of Dust, 1934

Scoop, 1938

Put Out More Flags, 1942

Work Suspended, 1942

Brideshead Revisited, 1945

Scott-King's Modern Europe, 1947

The Loved One, 1948

Helena, 1950

Men at Arms, 1952

Love Among the Ruins, 1953

Officers and Gentlemen, 1955

The Ordeal of Gilbert Pinfold, 1957

Unconditional Surrender, 1961

Basil Seal Rides Again, 1963

Sword of Honour, 1966 (a single volume version of
     Men at Arms, Officers and Gentlemen, and
     Unconditional Surrender)

The Complete Short Stories of Evelyn Waugh, 1998

POETRY, TRAVEL WRITING, AND OTHER NONFICTION

PRB: An Essay on the Pre-Raphaelite Brotherhood, 1926

Rossetti: His Life and Works, 1928

Labels, 1930

Remote People, 1931

Ninety-Two Days, 1934

Edmund Campion, 1935

Waugh in Abyssinia, 1936

Robbery Under the Law, 1939

When the Going Was Good, 1946

Wine in Peace and War, 1947

The Life of the Right Reverend Ronald Knox, 1959

A Tourist in Africa, 1960

A Little Learning (first volume of an autobiography, 1964)

DIARIES, LETTERS, AND ESSAYS

The Diaries of Evelyn Waugh, edited by Michael Davie,
    1976

The Letters of Evelyn Waugh, edited by Mark Amory, 1980

The Essays, Articles and Reviews of Evelyn Waugh,
    edited by Donat Gallagher, 1983

BIBLIOGRAPHY

Acton, Harold. *More Memories of an Aesthete*. London: Methuen, 1970.
————. *Nancy Mitford: A Memoir*. London: Hamish Hamilton, 1975.
Amory, Mark. *Lord Berners: The Last Eccentric*. London: Pimlico, 1999.
Balsan, Consuelo Vanderbilt. *The Glitter and the Gold*. New York: Harper, 1952.
Bowker, Gordon. *Inside George Orwell*. New York: Palgrave Macmillan, 2003.
Card, Tim. *Eton Renewed: A History from 1860 to the Present Day*. London: J. Murray, 1994.
Carpenter, Humphrey. *The Brideshead Generation: Evelyn Waugh and His Friends*. Boston: Houghton Mifflin, 1990.
Connolly, Cyril. *The Evening Colonnade*. London: David Bruce & Watson, 1973.
Courtney, Nicholas. *In Society: The Brideshead Years*. London: Pavilion, 1986.
Crick, Bernard. *George Orwell: A Life*. Boston: Little, Brown, 1980.
Donaldson, Frances. *Evelyn Waugh: Portrait of a Country Neighbour*. Philadelphia: Chilton, 1968.
Fyvel, T. R. *George Orwell: A Personal Memoir*. London: Hutchinson, 1983.
Gross, Miriam, ed. *The World of George Orwell*. New York: Simon & Schuster, 1971.
Guinness, Jonathan, with Catherine Guinness. *The House of Mitford*. New York: Viking, 1985.
Hastings, Selena. *Evelyn Waugh: A Biography*. Boston: Houghton Mifflin, 1994.
Hitchens, Christopher. *Why Orwell Matters*. New York: Basic Books, 2002.
Hollis, Christopher. *Evelyn Waugh*. London: Longmans, 1954.

————. *George Orwell: The Man and His Works*. Chicago: Regnery, 1956.

Huxley, Aldous. *Brave New World*. New York: HarperPerennial, 2006.

Ingle, Stephen. *George Orwell: A Political Life*. Manchester University Press, 1993.

Ishiguro, Kazuo. *The Remains of the Day*. New York: Vintage, 1993.

Korda, Michael. *Charmed Lives: A Family Romance*. New York: Perennial, 2002.

Larkin, Emma. *Finding George Orwell in Burma*. New York: Penguin, 2005.

Lovell, Mary S. *The Sisters: The Saga of the Mitford Family*. New York: W. W. Norton, 2001.

McCrum, Robert. *Wodehouse: A Life*. New York: W. W. Norton, 2004.

Meacham, Jon. *Franklin and Winston: An Intimate Portrait of an Epic Friendship*. New York: Random House, 2003.

Meyers, Jeffrey. *Orwell: Wintry Conscience of a Generation*. New York: W. W. Norton, 2000.

Mosley, Charlotte, ed. *The Mitfords: Letters Between Six Sisters*. New York: HarperCollins, 2007.

Nicolson, Juliet. *The Perfect Summer: England 1911, Just Before the Storm*. New York: Grove Press, 2006.

Patey, Douglas Lane. *The Life of Evelyn Waugh*. Oxford: Blackwell, 1998.

Powell, Anthony. *To Keep the Ball Rolling: The Memoirs of Anthony Powell*. University of Chicago Press, 1976.

Pryce-Jones, David, ed. *Cyril Connolly: Journal and Memoir*. New York: Ticknor & Fields, 1984.

————. *Evelyn Waugh and His World*. Boston: Little, Brown, 1973.

Routh, Guy. *Occupation and Pay in Great Britain, 1906–60*. Cambridge: The University Press, 1965.

Shelden, Michael. *Orwell: The Authorized Biography*. New York: HarperCollins, 1991.

Spurling, Hilary. *The Girl from the Fiction Department: A Portrait of Sonia Orwell*. New York: Counterpoint, 2002.

Stannard, Martin. *Evelyn Waugh: The Early Years 1903–1939*. New York: W. W. Norton, 1986.

————. *Evelyn Waugh: The Later Years 1939–1966.* New York: W. W. Norton, 1992.

Stansky, Peter, and William Abrahams. *Orwell: The Transformation.* New York: Knopf, 1980.

————. *The Unknown Orwell.* New York: Knopf, 1972.

Sykes, Christopher. *Evelyn Waugh: A Biography.* London: Collins, 1975.

Taylor, D. J. *Orwell: The Life.* New York: Henry Holt, 2003.

Wadhams, Stephen. *Remembering Orwell.* New York: Penguin, 1984.

Waugh, Alexander. *Fathers and Sons: The Autobiography of a Family.* New York: Nan A. Talese, 2007.

Waugh, Auberon. *Will This Do? The First Fifty Years of Auberon Waugh: An Autobiography.* New York: Carroll & Graf, 1998.

Waugh, Evelyn. *Black Mischief.* New York: Dell, 1961.

————. *The Letters of Evelyn Waugh and Diana Cooper.* Edited by Artemis Cooper. New York: Ticknor & Fields, 1992.

West, W. J., ed. *Orwell: The War Commentaries.* New York: Pantheon, 1985.

NOTES

PROLOGUE

xii "I read your books": Evelyn Waugh, *The Diaries of Evelyn Waugh*, ed. Michael Davie (Boston: Little, Brown, 1976), 318.

xii "There were two ambassadors": Ibid.

xii "Lunched at the Ritz": Ibid., 319.

xii–xiii (who "threw a cocktail"): Ibid., 315.

xiii A picnic: "Diana": Ibid., 326.

xiii "The party at tea": Ibid., 322.

xiii On that same balmy night: Bernard Crick, *George Orwell: A Life* (Boston: Little, Brown, 1980), 127.

xiii He, however, made the distinction: Ibid.

xiii "When you have shared a bed": George Orwell, *The Road to Wigan Pier* (New York: Harcourt, 1956), 133.

CHAPTER ONE | CUTTING CLASS

3 "Mr. Blair would walk": Stephen Wadhams, compiler, *Remembering Orwell* (Ontario; Harmondsworth: Penguin, 1984), 29.

4 "Old man Blair": Ibid., 29–30.

4 Eric Blair, as George Orwell: Orwell, *The Road to Wigan Pier*, 121.

7 The club would be closed to those: D. J. Taylor, *Orwell: The Life* (New York: Henry Holt, 2003), 107.

12 "In a world where": George Orwell, *The Collected Essays, Journalism and Letters of George Orwell*, eds. Sonia Orwell and Ian Angus (New York: Harcourt, Brace, 1968), 4:364.

12 For Eric Blair, the: Ibid., 359.

13 "How much a year": Ibid., 358.

13 Since his own: Ibid., 359–61.

13 "curious cult of Scotland": Ibid., 357.

15   "Daddy loves Alec": Selena Hastings, *Evelyn Waugh: A Biography* (Boston: Houghton Mifflin, 1994), 28.

15   When his nurse: Ibid., 22.

17   Upon being taught: Alexander Waugh, *Fathers and Sons* (New York: Nan A. Talese, 2007), 25.

18   One incident alone: Hastings, *Evelyn Waugh*, 104.

20   "a beautiful boy": Ibid., 44.

20   Beaton wrote to a friend: Ibid.

21   Wolfe said that the bullies: Tom Wolfe, in his contribution to the symposium "What Is a Liberal—Who Is a Conservative," *Commentary* 47, September 1976, 109–10.

21   portraying it in his short stories: Ibid., 49.

22   "I have never seen anything": Waugh, *Diaries*, 100.

CHAPTER TWO | AT THE BOTTOM OF THE HILL

26   "may have been not only": Humphrey Carpenter, *The Brideshead Generation: Evelyn Waugh and His Friends* (Boston: Houghton Mifflin, 1990), 17.

26   Openly homosexual: Waugh, *Diaries*, 797.

26   There was, for example: Ibid., 790.

26   If you had asked: Ibid., 793.

27   "As he himself ": Ibid.

27   And Henry Yorke: Carpenter, *The Brideshead Generation*, 482.

27   But the relative: Evelyn Waugh, *Brideshead Revisited* (Boston: Little, Brown, 1945), 41.

28   John le Carré, many years later: Jeffrey Meyers, *Orwell: Wintry Conscience of a Generation* (New York: W. W. Norton, 2000), 325.

30   The club had maintained: Carpenter, *The Brideshead Generation*, 76.

31   Since the point: Hastings, *Evelyn Waugh*, 100.

31   The neglect of his: Ibid., 99.

31   When Waugh translated: Carpenter, *The Brideshead Generation*, 65.

32   And so, when Cruttwell: Hastings, *Evelyn Waugh*, 86.

32   One day in a lecture: Carpenter, *The Brideshead Generation*, 68.

32   Waugh then proceeded: Ibid., 69.

33   Some spent thousands: Guy Routh, *Occupation and Pay in Great Britain, 1906–60* (Cambridge: The University Press, 1965), 64.

34   "It seemed as if ": Waugh, *Brideshead Revisited*, 45.

35   "Alone among the hundreds": Wilfrid Sheed, "Portrait of the Artist as a Self-Made Man," *The New York Review of Books*, December 16, 1993.

35   "I cannot say that": Hastings, *Evelyn Waugh*, 112.

37   "One night": Evelyn Waugh, *A Little Learning* (Boston: Little, Brown, 1964), 229–30.

38   At about this time: Tim Card, *Eton Renewed: A History from 1860 to the Present Day* (London: J. Murray, 1994), 161.

40   "Write a letter to a relative": Peter Stansky and William Abrahams, *The Unknown Orwell* (New York: Knopf, 1972), 154.

41   He traveled with servants: Ibid., 180.

42   But it was a desperately lonely: Ibid., 184–85.

42   Once, when Blair: Ibid., 188.

43   Later he wrote: Ibid., 201.

CHAPTER THREE | MR. TOAD ON TOP

46   "I fell in love": Waugh, *A Little Learning*, 216.

46   "Her maternal grandmother": Hastings, *Evelyn Waugh*, 125.

47   When Olivia or her mother: Ibid.

48   When she heard: Ibid., 127.

48   Even the newspaper: Ibid., 132.

49   Apparently the only time: Ibid., 150–51.

50   "Mr. Toad on Top": Ibid., 157.

51   She had already: Ibid., 156.

52   so favorably impressed: Ibid., 166.

57   They were married in Berlin: Mary S. Lovell, *The Sisters: The Saga of the Mitford Family* (New York: W. W. Norton, 2001), 211.

57   "The greatest moment": Ibid., 206.

58   At age fifteen: Nicholas Courtney, *In Society: The Brideshead Years* (London: Pavilion, 1986), 139.

58   "Oh Seer Enry": Ibid.

58   "Elizabeth Ponsonby": Ibid., 38.

59   In July 1928: Ibid., 148–49.

59   On the eve: Ibid., 144.

59   (Oliver Messel went): Ibid., 147.

60   There was, in fact: Ibid., 140–42.

60   In his book: Ibid., 138.

61   "Mixed parties": Evelyn Waugh, *Vile Bodies* (New York: Dell, 1958), 106.

62   "So the last Earl": Ibid., 92.

62   "People bought the book": Martin Stannard, *Evelyn Waugh: The Early Years* (New York: W. W. Norton, 1986), 204.

63   He recorded: Waugh, *Diaries,* 309.

63   "I didn't know that it was": Evelyn Waugh, *The Letters of Evelyn Waugh,* ed. Mark Amory (New Haven, Conn.: Ticknor & Fields, 1980), 39.

65   Five years: Evelyn Waugh, *A Handful of Dust* (New York: Dell, 1963), 120–21.

67   "We've never had such laughs": Lovell, *The Sisters,* 505.

68   And sure enough: Hastings, *Evelyn Waugh,* 225–26.

69   When Waugh was a boy: Ibid., 39.

69   "The shallowness of my early piety": Evelyn Waugh, *The Essays, Articles and Reviews of Evelyn Waugh,* ed. Donat Gallagher (Boston: Little, Brown, 1983), 366.

69   "Those of you": Ibid., 367.

72   Since Nazi Germany: Hastings, *Evelyn Waugh,* 328.

72   Waugh wrote to: *The Letters of Evelyn Waugh and Diana Cooper,* ed. Artemis Cooper (New York: Ticknor & Fields, 1992), 51.

72   Perhaps more impressive: Hastings, *Evelyn Waugh,* 352.

73   "I thought we'd heard": Waugh, *Diaries,* 407n2.

73   The announcement in *The Times:* Hastings, *Evelyn Waugh,* 356.

CHAPTER FOUR | LOVE FINDS ERIC BLAIR

76   One young lady: Taylor, *Orwell,* 91.

76   "Inside the park": Ibid.

76   He wrote two novels: Ibid., 94.

76   He had picked up: Ibid., 98.

77   Many of his: Ibid., 181.

77   In London he: Ibid., 113.

78   Gollancz helped Blair: Ibid., 126.

78   He wrote another novel: Ibid., 139.

78   His average income: Ibid., 151.

78   He did not permit: Ibid., 124.

79   She was never: Ibid., 159.

79   She saw at once: Ibid.

79   At the same time, Evelyn Waugh: Hastings, *Evelyn Waugh*, 254.

79   When Orwell proposed: Taylor, *Orwell*, 62.

80   The only rational: Ibid., 184.

81   Though visiting friends: Ibid., 189.

81   She once said: Ibid., 159–60.

84   They widely circulated: Ibid., 224.

85   She arranged for him: Ibid., 228.

85   But when she leaned over: Ibid., 230.

CHAPTER FIVE | THE WAUGH TO END ALL WAUGHS

89   So on September 1: Waugh, *Diaries*, 439.

90   And when it did come: Ibid.

90   "The future must be": Orwell, *Collected Essays*, 2:345.

91   "There is a symbolic difference": Waugh, *Diaries*, 438.

93   He had an interview: Ibid., 446.

93   The doctor couldn't help: Ibid., 451.

93   "A colonel in khaki": Ibid.

94   The second was Brendan Bracken: Ibid., 449.

94   On hearing that: Anthony Powell, *To Keep the Ball Rolling: The Memoirs of Anthony Powell* (University of Chicago Press, 1976), 72.

94   Though few would have: The Earl of Birkenhead, "Fiery Particles," chap. 11 in *Evelyn Waugh and His World*, ed. David Pryce-Jones (Boston: Little, Brown, 1973), 139.

95   When Waugh was denied: Sykes, *Evelyn Waugh*, 229.

96   He was permitted to: Waugh, *Diaries*, 368–69.

97   While Randolph was serving: Jon Meacham, *Franklin and Winston: An Intimate Portrait of an Epic Friendship* (New York: Random House, 2003), 173.

97   In a recent biography: Christopher Ogden, *Life of the Party: The Biography of Pamela Digby Churchill Hayward Harriman* (Boston: Little, Brown, 1994), after 184.

98   The most honest: Waugh, *Diaries,* 587.

99   They stopped on the way: Ibid., 570.

100 "My father was master": Waugh, *Brideshead Revisited,* 68–70.

100 Earlier in the war: Hastings, *Evelyn Waugh,* 466.

101 "Tito like Lesbian": Ibid.

101 Thereafter, he referred: Earl of Birkenhead, "Fiery Particles," 150–51.

101 Ominously, the Waugh diary: Waugh, *Diaries,* 574–75.

102 But numerous banquets: Ibid., 581.

103 The pages grow: Ibid., 589.

103 "I should like": Ibid., 582.

103 "The facts are": Ibid., 587.

103 And there was something: Ibid.

104 He had much to describe: Earl of Birkenhead, "Fiery Particles," 143–44.

105 One evening, as Birkenhead: Ibid., 150.

106 The decisive confrontation: Ibid., 151–52.

107 "But Randolph soon began": Ibid., 161.

107 He issued a military order: Ibid.

108 By this time Birkenhead, too: Ibid., 161–62.

109 He left with anxiety: Ibid., 163.

110 And when Randolph became: Waugh, *Letters of Waugh and Cooper,* 307.

CHAPTER SIX | THE HOME FIRES BURNING

111 The Home Guard was organized: Orwell, *Collected Essays,* 2:151.

112 Cyril Connolly said: Cyril Connolly, *The Evening Colonnade* (London: David Bruce & Watson, 1973), 382–83.

112 Remembering the fierce: Orwell, *Collected Essays,* 2:153.

112   He wrote an article: Crick, *George Orwell,* 270–71.

113   Because of his experience: Meyers, *Orwell,* 201.

114   Eileen was beside herself: Ibid.

114   He once loaded the wrong: Ibid.

115   The first significant outlet: Crick, *George Orwell,* 265.

116   This work was time-consuming: Meyers, *Orwell,* 213.

116   a small but increasingly influential: Ibid., 460.

117   In an essay about: Orwell, *Collected Essays,* 1:450.

117   Orwell concludes: Ibid., 460.

117   Orwell argued that: Ibid., 518–19.

118   "The thing that": Ibid., 531–32.

118   Unfettered by any: Ibid., 2:13.

118   Even the titles: Ibid., 535.

118   "Reading Mr. Malcolm": Ibid., 15.

119   He liked Aldous Huxley's: Ibid., 17.

119   "It is not certain": Ibid., 79.

119   So Orwell's blunt: Ibid., 105.

120   In 1942, Orwell: Ibid., 209.

120   He didn't think: Ibid., 309.

120   He asked despairingly: Ibid., 259.

121   On why totalitarianism: Ibid., 107.

121   "It is commonly said": Ibid., 44.

121   "England is a family": Ibid., 84.

121   Rich young people: Ibid., 315.

121   "A humanitarian is": Ibid., 187.

121   "We live in": Ibid., 332–33.

121   "No one is": Ibid., 365.

121   "Saints should always": Ibid., 4:463.

122   He infuriated: Ibid., 91.

122   British pacifists were: Ibid., 2:89.

122   He shocked everyone: Ibid., 3:159.

122   He even defended: Ibid., 224.

123   It contains a perfect: Crick, *George Orwell,* 267.

124   This beat out: Ibid., 147.

124   because he was head: Ibid., 181.

125   And then he did: Ibid., 312–13.

126   The agent sent: Ibid., 313.

126   The high official: Gordon Bawker, *Inside George Orwell* (New York: Palgrave Macmillan, 2003), 312.

127   There was also Faber: Crick, *George Orwell*, 314.

127   But then he opened: Ibid., 315.

128   (He had even): Ibid., 317.

128   By the time: *The New York Times*, May 28, 1981.

CHAPTER SEVEN | YES, WE HAVE NO BANANAS

131   Her full name: Teresa Waugh D'Arms, interview with author, Ann Arbor, Michigan, October 4, 2006.

132   Auberon Waugh's son: Alexander Waugh, *Fathers and Sons: The Autobiography of a Family* (New York: Nan Talese, 2007), 273.

132   Indeed, the *Oxford:* Ibid.

132   The insatiability of: Ibid., 276.

134   When Alexander Korda: Michael Korda, *Charmed Lives: A Family Romance* (New York: Perennial, 2002), 147.

134   She brought the bananas home: Auberon Waugh, *Will This Do? The First Fifty Years of Auberon Waugh* (New York: Carroll & Graf, 1998), 67.

135   However, Auberon's elder: D'Arms, interview.

136   Out on patrol: Waugh, *Fathers and Sons*, 359–60.

136   The fame of his father: *The Daily Mail*, as quoted in Waugh, *Fathers and Sons*, 361.

137   Apparently it was: Martin Stannard, *Evelyn Waugh: The Later Years 1939–1966* (New York: W. W. Norton, 1992), 408.

137   When he was courting: Waugh, *Letters*, 104.

138   August 24, 1946: Waugh, *Diaries*, 658.

138   December 23, 1946: Ibid., 667.

138   April 19, 1947: Ibid., 676.

139   "My two eldest": Waugh, *Letters*, 217.

140   In the same diary: Waugh, *Diaries*, 668.

140   He scrawled a letter: Waugh, *Fathers and Sons*, 369.

141   Waugh disliked: Ibid., 251.

142   He saw his children: D'Arms, interview.

142   Orwell concluded: Taylor, *Orwell*, 335.

143   He loved his wife: Ibid.

143   They named him: Meyers, *Orwell*, 228.

143   While he had: Taylor, *Orwell*, 336.

143   He even considered: T. R. Fyvel, *George Orwell: A Personal Memoir* (London: Hutchinson, 1983), 168–69.

144   One thing bothered him: Meyers, *Orwell*, 233–34.

145   "I hear that": Taylor, *Orwell*, 345.

145   She had tumors: Ibid., 345–46.

145   Orwell learned: Meyers, *Orwell*, 237.

146   Always honest: Ibid., 238.

146   He found a dream: Ibid.

147   Jura has been called: Ibid., 256.

147   "a cross between": Ibid., 258.

147   He had hemorrhaged: Ibid., 245.

148   David Astor was: Ibid., 210.

149   "Lady Astor": Consuelo Vanderbilt, Balsan, *The Glitter and the Gold* (New York: Harper, 1952), 204–5.

149   The house that: Meyers, *Orwell*, 258.

150   "I liked living": Wadhams, *Remembering Orwell*, 193.

150   Orwell had been hostile: Taylor, *Orwell*, 378.

151   Everyone who saw: Wadhams, *Remembering Orwell*, 189.

151   These inconveniences took: Ibid., 188.

152   Off the northern coast: Ibid., 189.

152   He decided one day: Ibid.

153   "Curious thing about seals": Ibid., 190.

153   So the cold, wet: Ibid., 192.

153   The desperately sick: Ibid., 200.

154   The only friend: Ibid., 211.

154   Despite his terrible: Ibid., 199.

155   "It's a strange feeling": Ibid., 148.

CHAPTER EIGHT | THE MEETING

158   He wrote for: Robert McCrum, *Wodehouse: A Life* (New York: W. W. Norton, 2004), 124–41.

158   (Upon arriving there): Ibid., 285.

159   Early in 1945: Orwell, *Collected Essays*, 3:341.

159   He regarded Wodehouse: Frances Donaldson, *Evelyn Waugh: Portrait of a Country Neighbour* (Philadelphia: Chilton, 1968), 73.

159   He must have been: Orwell, *Collected Essays*, 3:353.

160   In *The Tablet:* Waugh, *Essays*, 304–7.

160   Waugh replied: Waugh, *Letters*, 210.

161   As he told: Waugh, *Diaries*, 633.

162   An exemplary person: Waugh, *Essays*, 306.

162   But, putting religion: Ibid., 307.

162   "English writers at forty": Waugh, *Diaries*, 560.

164   A meal in Paris: Waugh, *Brideshead Revisited*, 173.

164   Intimation of romance: Ibid., 76.

164   Explaining the disdain: Ibid., 210.

164   (When Waugh's daughter): D'Arms, interview.

166   "I can't marry you": Waugh, *Brideshead Revisited*, 340.

166   He wrote a friend: George Orwell, *The Complete Works of George Orwell*, ed. Peter Davison (London: Secker & Warburg, 1998), 19:400.

168   In an anonymously: Ibid., 417.

169   When Waugh wrote: Ibid., 20:44.

169   "The modern world": Ibid., 45–46.

172   "Within the last few": Orwell, *Complete Works*, 20:74.

173   "Though the approach": Ibid., 76.

173   Orwell was too sick: Ibid., 19:417.

173   In describing the: Ibid., 20:77.

173   One note refers: Ibid., 79.

174   "I recall him saying": Fyvel, *George Orwell*, 167–68.

174   Today, in the harsh: Emma Larkin, *Finding George Orwell in Burma* (New York: Penguin, 2005), 10–11.

175   He did manage to hide: Taylor, *Orwell*, 407.

177   "You see how much": Ibid.

178   And so it was: Ibid., 408.

179   He did mention: Ibid.

179   In a subsequent article: Malcolm Muggeridge, "A Knight of the Woeful Countenance," in *The World of George Orwell*, ed. Miriam Gross (New York: Simon & Schuster, 1971), 173.

CHAPTER NINE | THE SAME MAN

181   "At fifty": Orwell, *Collected Essays*, 515.
181   Only his eyes: Harold Acton, *More Memoirs of an Aesthete* (London: Methuen, 1970), 152.
182   (Indeed, the coatroom): Waugh, *Diaries*, 773.
184   "The common people": Orwell, *Collected Essays*, 3:223.
186   In Waugh's great: Evelyn Waugh, *Men at Arms* (Boston: Little, Brown, 1952), 7–8.
187   Orwell's *1984* is: Aldous Huxley, *Brave New World* (New York: HarperPerennial), 2006.
190   The first paragraph: George Orwell, *1984* (New York: Signet Classic, 1984), 201.
191   In an essay on: Orwell, *Collected Essays*, 4:178.
192   He had written hopefully: Ibid., 2:77.
193   A perfect example: Kazuo Ishiguro, *The Remains of the Day* (New York: Vintage), 1993.
194   "My good man": Ibid., 195–96.
195   "A modern literary": Orwell, *Collected Essays*, 4:409.
196   He felt that the code: Ibid., 215.
197   In fact, when William: Waugh, *Letters*, 536.
198   Orwell, stunned at: Orwell, *Collected Essays*, 4:179–80.
198   Before their marriage: Lovell, *The Sisters*, 152–53.
199   "Every year or so": Waugh, *Black Mischief* (New York: Dell, 1961), 257.
199   On arrival he is: Ibid., 278.
199   So Seth quickly makes: Ibid., 283–84.
200   Allocation to one: Orwell, *1984*, 208.
200   It is, as Orwell: Orwell, *Collected Essays*, 4:179.
200   This is the: Ibid., 3:156.
200   He also wrote: Ibid., 36.
201   "Orthodoxies, whether": Ibid., 12.
201   He saw that: Ibid., 2:265.
201   He wrote, as we have: Waugh, *Essays*, 367.
202   In fact, when Orwell: Orwell, *Collected Essays*, 3:243–44.
202   Orwell scoffed at: Ibid., 4:212.

202   "One must choose": Ibid., 299.

203   He saw the need: Ibid., 3:102.

203   Orwell believed: Ibid., 2:14.

203   "It was nearly": Waugh, *Essays,* 103–4.

205   If George Orwell: Orwell, *Essays,* 4:127.

205   As an example Orwell: Ibid., 136.

206   In this regard: Ibid., 3:384.

206   "In a few deft": Evelyn Waugh, *Scoop* (New York: Dell, 1961), 18.

208   An excellent example: Louis Menand, "After Elvis," *The New Yorker,* October 26, 1998, 164.

209   Orwell observed: Orwell, *Essays,* 3:139.

EPILOGUE

213   In announcing his death: Crick, *Orwell,* 405.

213   His will: Ibid., 404.

213   The cemetery chosen: Meyers, *Orwell,* 312.

213   "G. Orwell is dead": Waugh, *Letters,* 320.

214   She ensured that Richard: Bowker, *Inside George Orwell,* 426.

215   She died without: Hilary Spurling, *The Girl from the Fiction Department: A Portrait of Sonia Orwell* (New York: Counterpoint, 2002), 175.

215   Richard Blair was raised: Taylor, *Orwell,* 420.

215   In 1964, he married: Orwell, *Collected Works,* 20: appendix 13, 307.

216   (He would have had): Hastings, *Evelyn Waugh,* 515–16.

216   He was interviewed: Martin Stannard, *Evelyn Waugh: The Later Years 1939–1966* (New York: W. W. Norton, 1992), 336.

216   When asked his opinion: Ibid., 337.

216   "There are individual men and women": Sykes, *Evelyn Waugh,* 356.

216   When the interviewer: Ibid.

217   In 1956 the Waugh family: Hastings, *Evelyn Waugh,* 582.

218   He coveted a knighthood: Stannard, *Later Years,* 415.

INDEX

PHOTOGRAPH INSERT
CREDITS

LITTLE ERIC BLAIR: George Orwell Archive, UCL Library Services, Special Collections

YOUNG EVELYN WAUGH: Lancing College Archives

ERIC BLAIR FISHING: Courtesy of Dione Venables / Guiniver Buddicom Estate

THE SWIMMING POOL AT ST. CYPRIAN'S: George Orwell Archive, UCL Library Services, Special Collections

THE HOUSE IN GOLDERS GREEN: Private Collection

RICHARD BLAIR: George Orwell Archive, UCL Library Services, Special Collections

ERIC BLAIR AT ETON: Hills and Saunders / Reproduced by permission of the Provost and Fellows of Eton College

EVELYN WAUGH VISITING OXFORD: Private Collection

CRUTTWELL: National Portrait Gallery, London

THE POLICE TRAINING SCHOOL: George Orwell Archive, UCL Library Services, Special Collections

THE BRIGHT YOUNG PEOPLE: © Topham / The Image Works

EVELYN GARDNER WAUGH: Private Collection

PORTRAIT OF EVELYN WAUGH: *Portrait of Evelyn Waugh*, 1930, by Henry Lamb / Private Collection / The Bridgeman Art Library / The Estate of Henry Lamb.

SHE-EVELYN AND HE-EVELYN: © Mary Evans Picture Library / The Image Works

EILEEN O'SHAUGHNESSY: George Orwell Archive, UCL Library Services, Special Collections

ON THE ARAGON FRONT: George Orwell Archive, UCL Library
Services, Special Collections

LAURA HERBERT: Photo by J. A. Hampton / Topical Press Agency /
Hulton Archive / Getty Images

TOP OF THE HILL: Private Collection

THE STORES: George Orwell Archive, UCL Library Services, Special
Collections

WAUGH IN UNIFORM: Howard Coster, National Portrait Gallery,
London

ORWELL AND T. S. ELIOT: © BBC Photo Library

WAUGH AND RANDOLPH CHURCHILL: Private Collection

EILEEN WITH BABY: George Orwell Archive, UCL Library Services,
Special Collections

ROAD TO BARNHILL: George Orwell Archive, UCL Library Services,
Special Collections

ORWELL WITH RICHARD: Photo by Vernon Richards / George Orwell
Archive, UCL Library Services, Special Collections

WAUGH WRITING: Mark Gerson / Camera Press / Retna

ORWELL WRITING: Photo by Vernon Richards / George Orwell
Archive, UCL Library Services, Special Collections

WAUGH FAMILY: Harry Ransom Humanities Research Center,
The University of Texas at Austin

LAURA WAUGH: AP Images

SONIA BROWNELL: George Orwell Archive, UCL Library Services,
Special Collections

WAUGH IN FRONT OF HIS HOME: Mark Gerson / Camera Press / Retna

DAVID LEBEDOFF is the award-winning author of five books, including *Cleaning Up*, about the *Exxon Valdez* case, and *The Uncivil War: How a New Elite Is Destroying Our Democracy*. Lebedoff is a graduate of the University of Minnesota and Harvard Law School. He lives in Minneapolis with his wife and three children.

This book is set in Fournier, a typeface named for Pierre-Simon Fournier, the youngest son of a French printing family. He started out engraving woodblocks and large capitals, then moved on to fonts of type. In 1736 he began his own foundry and made several important contributions in the field of type design; he is said to have cut 147 alphabets of his own creation. Fournier is probably best remembered as the designer of St. Augustine Ordinaire, a face that served as the model for Monotype's Fournier, which was released in 1925.